Table of Contents

ISBN: 978-1-312-23056-9
Publish: Lulu Press, Inc.

MOVING FORWARD: But Knowing the Rules of the Game to Love

Kenneth Brown

Dedication

Lord Jesus thank you for guiding me and allowing me to follow you on this journey called life. You have tested my strength, my heart, my will and my ability to remain sane. But I was and am ok with that, because I know you are only making me a stronger soldier for your battle. I want to thank my family and friends for inspiration. Thank you to all my loyal readers.

Follow me on:

FACEBOOK: @LikeKennethB
TWITTER: @LikeKennethB
ABOUTME.COM/BrownKenneth

Table of Contents

POEMS

Introduction

Why Moving Forward: But knowing the Rules to this Game of love. In my book I explain how deep down I really believe that everything in our lives is directly affected by how much we love ourselves. I am excited to have come up with my own analogy in the form of rules, that I feel really pulls it all together. Sharing my life experience in hopes that others can explore and expand on this concept with me.

I started writing as part of my own private attempt to change the world. It wouldn't feel or be right if I could not express myself. That's why I wanted to share my collection of poetry and short stories with others. Writing stories with real people in mind. People who love and hate and sometimes even have sex for all the wrong reasons. Knowing in mind that it really is possible to make a difference, no matter how small you may think. That's why erotica to me is an art form expressing an individual's thoughts in a way like no other. Each reader will always take something different from your contribution. My urban gay community has a way of understanding me in, in ways only we know. Admitting that we do come together behind closed doors to be comfortable in our skins to express and talk about our problems together. That's why I wanted my stories to wrench the soul. Open the mind to feel my love, my pain and to teach us to support in the cause and our relationship with each other. Maybe my words might counsel you into coming to grips with anger, fear and pain, that's behind our behavior in our way of living.

Let me ask you this question. Have you ever been in love? Have you notice that love will have you do crazy things? And by crazy, I mean over act, trigger obsessive behavior, make you feel impulsive, and create a lot of jealousy. Being in love can be a blessing and a curse. I'm usually the strong one to hold it together, never the one to complain, but after I had experience so much pain and loss in my life. I realize that it truly affected me. So, it made me put up this wall to protect me from others or anything that would try to come in my life to tear me down. Which explains these rules I set for myself? There are millions of rules that we all can come up with, when it comes to the rules of love and trying to implement them into our lives. We all have a story to tell. But I wanted to share just 12 of my rules from my journal to show how we dismiss the red flags in our lives, turning a blind eye to the signs, not realizing that eventually they'll come back to haunt you. In the end, you end up hurt and resentful. If we only listen to our hearts and catch on to the signs, then maybe we could have protected ourselves from the negative people that cross our paths.

Let's remember that there is a process when you're dating or even in a long-term relationship that requires negotiation and a clear communication. Love is often challenge by change, but it does provide a variety of opportunities for us to grow as individuals.

Don't be fool by the book cover. The positive side of me wants to believe that there is still hope for us single folks to someday find our soul mate. Love matters, love works. Whether it's a romantic kind of love or the emotional bond between yourself, your partner, family or friends. Learning how to love yourself is a key ingredient of happiness. Self-love is at the very core of our well-being, self-empowerment and our ability to enjoy the kind of life we want. Even if you had everything else in your life exactly the way you want it, you wouldn't be able to enjoy it, if you weren't at peace with yourself. Think about every relationship you ever had with someone, who exactly mirrors one or more aspects of the relationship with yourself. Your emotions, your traits, and your feelings are reflected at you from other people either through in-kind responses or through predictable reactions to the emotions or feelings that you're issuing. Perhaps you might feel condescension, radiant low self-esteem, irritability or dismissiveness toward another person, which lowers your estimation of them and causes you to treat them less seriously, yet in doing so, you ignore the fact that they reflect your negative appraisal of them. Learning to see yourself as other see you, is an important way of breaking this unconscious bind and injecting balance into our lives by seeking to give the best of ourselves and to mirror back the best of others.

My rules of the game to love will help you think of your own rules, but also help you benefit from the simple principles of forming and sustaining a strong, enduring and ultimately life enhancing your relationship if you're in a relationship or just single weighing your options to decide to give love a try and date again.

IM NOT CRAZY

I'm not crazy.
I'm not giving into these psychotic and evil bitches.
I'm not giving them what they want.

Truth is; Before you diagnose yourself with depression or low self-esteem, first make sure that you are not, in fact just surrounded by assholes.

This is a mad world.
In this life, to earn your place you must fight for it.

Caring doesn't make you weak, it makes you stronger.
But letting your guard down, leaving yourself vulnerable is.
Not caring what other people think is the best choice you will ever make. It is something you must remember.

Like all, my mind is filled with worries and fears I can't seem to release.
I dream of days without these tortured thoughts.
Enough is enough and I'm tired of the bullshit.
The lies, the deceit, the betrayal.
Not everyone is blessed with mental and moral support.

Shit! I'm not crazy! I just don't like what I see.
I'm not giving into these psychotic and evil bitches.
I'm not giving them what they want.
Now I can admit. I'm falling deeper into what I fear most.
Emptiness, Confusion, Isolation between me and them.
Fake friends, back stabbers behind my back.

Shit! Tell me the truth.
Are you a fake friend and leech for personal gain?
Where was you at on this rollercoaster journey of mines?
I was supportive and there for you.

Are you real or fake Bitch?
I have enough liars, poser, freak and cheaters.
Stabbing me in my back right now.
Selling me out for a yard or less.

Here me out when I say this.
Hell is an option for a crazy bitch.
So much pain, creativity lost, tortured thoughts from one owns problems. I don't like what I see
I'm tired of people who play mind games because of their insecurities.
You mad because, I exhibit confidence and success.

It was a struggle, but I overcame by myself.
I made it the right way, with no short cuts & lies.
You Bitches will do anything to get underneath my skin.
But am a child of destiny. And you are the devil's spawn sent to play mind games.
These scaffolding disguise as a Confidants, Constituents or Comrades. You can't tell anymore.

Life is 10% what happens to you and 90% how you react to it. So, Bitch I guess I'm reacting.
Can I share all my thoughts and not have you used them against me?
Because you sure won't be there when I need you the most.
Truth is; We are all messy.
As much as we put on a fake ass smile.
The world's a stage and were all actors auditioning for a role in people's lives, that no one ask for.
So what role are you playing with me today?

Let my intuition be a guide to Truth.
Be careful who you tell your secrets & dreams to.
Silly bitch! Tricks are really for kids.

No! You're not crazy & deep down your gut tells you who your real friends are.
And it's not the ones who been testing you lately with these head strong personalities & opinions you never ask for.

No! I'm not crazy.
I'm not giving into these psychotic and evil bitches.
I'm not giving them what they want.
My solution to my life's problem, the universe and everything in it.
Mind your own business, create your own lane and stay in it.

MOVING FORWARD- ENDNOTES

Living in a world filled with deceit and betrayal makes it hard for us to trust, therefore making it even harder for us to build friendships or be in a relationship. But when people show you their character one time, believe them the first time. #IMNOTCRAZY

OLD MEMORIES

In my mind I know it isn't fair.
I've lost so much in my life.
Sitting going through old letters.
Containing so many secrets from my past.

Flashbacks of familiar faces.
Reminding me of so much love and pain.
Old memories. Ok bits and pieces of past trueloves.
Some of them unclear.
If only I can feel there touch again. As clear as I would see my reflection in a mirror.

Dwelling over a past ex or relationship can be toxic.
I'm unable to let go. Why can't I let go?

Memories flow through me like air passing on a cold winter breeze, feeling cold.
Who's there to console me in my time of need
Secretly crying behind closed doors, never heard.

Obsessive Rumination and longing might be common in some people, but it's still can be problematic.
Maybe it's a fear of being single. Maybe my current thoughts are linked to obsessions about my past loves.
We say we don't care and pretend to move on.
But our problems are suppressed & hidden for the moment.

Lord, Jesus. Calling on Christ to fix my life.
I'm all over the place. Trying to cope.
Not realizing that it can be hard on the body, mind and spirit.

What I'm I doing?
I'm trying to do what's best for me.
My way of healing and dealing with my problems.

Humans have a strong need to belong
The thoughts of being desirable by someone may provide comfort in the face of a deteriorating relationship.
Even the best relationships have its ups and down.
This isn't fair. Life's not fair.

This depression weighs heavy on me. That's it.
Moving on isn't easy, as I'm sure you know.
My thoughts are slowly weighing heavy on me.

I'm not crazy.
I just haven't found a way through this pain and it feels like I ran into a brick wall and it has my faith shaken.
But one thing to remember.
You must create your own opportunity and walk on your own, because you will not find a ready-made path.
Nothings never free and it's not cheap to reach the ultimate realization of the truth.
Healing takes courage and we all have courage even if we must dig a little to find it.
I always knew looking back on the tears would make me laugh, but I never knew looking back on the laughs would make me cry.
But I do know, the only thing that remains.
Are my letters and bits and pieces of memories of the past?
Cherish and lock away forever.
As a caution reminder.

Chapter One

Rule #1. SELF-LOVE: Learning to love and put yourself first before getting into a relationship.

Before we discuss self-love, self-control and the single life. Let's define the love that we really want. Everybody wants to feel loved! We wanted to experience romance. We want a person that gives advice, support and in return we give them the same. But living happy in the present moment with oneself is the key I believe. Your interactions with the world and those around you, your thoughts and how you interpret events, relationships, actions and words is the one lesson we all need to learn. Because it all depends on how much you love to take care of yourself, which shapes the kind of life you live.

Now I'm not saying that were all meant to be alone. I just think were meant to accomplish several amazing things and deal with some very difficult things in our lives, probably alone before Mr./Mrs. Right comes along. Oftentimes we jump into a relationship when were not ready. No one is perfect, we all have certain flaws that we would like to change and work on. But if you want a 75% chance of having a successful relationship. Work on you first; i.e.; like your health, career, finances, mental issues etc. Whatever the reason is just fix it before bringing that extra baggage into a relationship. That's my opinion from life experience. I see people all the time trying to force a relationship with a lot of baggage dragging them down. Baby! That's a full- time job trying to give a person your time and energy and fix your problems too. When you meet your soul mate you want to come together to build a foundation and life without your single drama setbacks.

If we are truly honest with ourselves and want to keep it real. I think a lot of people have the LL Syndrome. Love vs Lust Syndrome. You can't forget the fact when you meet someone. That initial attraction stirs up neurotransmitters and hormones that create this excitement of infatuation and make you have a strong desire to be close and sexual with a person. Baby! That's not love. These chemicals and our emotional and psychological makeup can cause us to obfuscate reality and idealize the object of our attraction. Our time spent in a fantasy world lusting over people we want fuels our craving to be with him or her even more.

I bet your thinking actions speaks louder than words "isn't just a cliché". But when it's purely lust, were not too interested in spending time together without sex or the expectation of it. The Truth is; you can be completely ignorant to the fact that one person has development feelings for someone. But think about this. How long have you really known them? Is that truly love? Or are your hormones creating this strong desire of lust.

You know what that's the secret is? The simple truth; if you aspire to accomplish your dreams, to have freedom to be yourself, to challenge conformity and traditionally typical ways of living, you will never be able to live a fulfilling life unless you rid yourself from low self-esteem and acquire the courage of self-confidence. Funny thing is we are born with an innate sense of wanting to belong. Comparison is one of the biggest obstacles in finding self-esteem. We use it to find another standard of perfection for acceptance. Through social media sites like Facebook, Instagram etc., we constantly use our friends, family and colleagues to measured up to their financial success, or how happy our lives are compared to their, or at least what they choose to share. But we see only the small surface of other people's lives, and we assume we know all the imperfection of ours, yet we use this false surface perfection as a guideline of how well we are doing. Creating our own unreal image of perfection that we don't managed to live up to ourselves. Realizing our own imperfection, we begin to reject ourselves.

Listen, I'm an introvert masquerading around as an extrovert. At one point I did have low self-esteem and had this strong desire to belong. It was more like self-abuse; which came in many shapes and forms like; thinking negative, overeating, physical self-harm etc. At some point in my life it became misery and it took me awhile to go from self-abuse to self-confidence. It wasn't always like this, but I found peace in just enjoying my own company. You might not agree; you might even think something's wrong with me for wanting to be alone. But before I diagnose myself with depression or low self-esteem, first I had to make sure that I was not in fact, just surrounded by assholes. I love being indoors writing, reading a delightful book or watching tv with to some healthy food all by myself. That's my way of experiencing self-love and being genuine to myself. By respecting and accepting whoever that is. I refuse to sell my integrity, the pride we have in ourselves, to be someone more acceptable to others by gossiping, embracing silly cultural trends of fashion, drugs, gangs and negative mentalities.

Like if I get invited out with friends, I prefer some place quiet instead of the clubs where we can talk. I get valued from my relationships by getting to know you much more than just being around you. Healthy social interactions is good because it allowed me to be focused on what I need and turn away from automatic behavior patterns that get you into trouble, keep you stuck in the past and lesson self-love. And if you're an extrovert, don't assume there's no value in this for you. In big groups you may find that you can enjoy yourself even out in bars and clubs. Handling both situations well, is beautiful and important. But for me being able to happily conduct myself alone is an important part of being alone. I had to set boundaries and limits or say no to work, love or activities that deplete or harm me physically, emotionally and spiritually or express poorly who I am. Its starts there first. And its where I see a lot of people fail at. There scared of being alone and have a fear of dying alone and not finding anyone. Some think its self-sabotaging and that I fear love. Nope! There is no fear mechanism here. I'm on the same quest for love like you. I'm just not trying to control it. I'm trying to enjoy myself, but just single on it now. If you understand your good enough all by yourself and that it really is a choice. Believe me you can find anyone and spend time with them when you stop trying to force it to happen on your time. When everything is clear about our lives and you know the direction you want to take, I believe Mr. or Mrs. Right will appear when it's right and when you least expect it. I believe that happens when were most happy and fulfilled. Remember being alone and happy doesn't mean sequestering yourself from the world. It means being confident enough to know that you can surround yourself with good people or be in positive relationship if you want, but not depend on them for your own happiness.

Don't just date someone because you don't want to be alone. Use that precious time to learn about yourself and work on personal growth. All of us experience major and minor life challenges. How we handle these struggles daily determine our physical, as well as mental well-being and how it determine the kind of person we want to date or be in a relationship with. Sometimes it takes only a single event to convince us we have no control over our circumstances and that those challenges can consume us. But all life challenges have a direct relationship in defining our purpose in life. If only we could find assurance that there was a plan or reason for the difficulties, we face. Because dating can be an emotional confusing whirlwind. Especially in the LGBT Community.

I think we as gay men should apply the 90-day rules too, just like women if you're seriously looking for a partner. I say that because were still fighting a long history to end racism, prejudice, discrimination and the stigma on HIV/AIDS in this world. This is an issue I hold dear to my heart.

There's still a lack of education, discrimination, fear, panic, issues and lies being spread amongst individuals in our community. I think people make stereotyped assumptions about our sexuality. And I believe one of the biggest ways to fight stigma and empower HIV- positive people is by speaking out openly safely and honestly about who we are and what we experience.

Dating can be very tricky for anyone, but if you are living with HIV, you have some extra things to think about. Two important things to consider are; whom do I date (a positive or negative person)? Or When do I tell him/her? If we apply the 90-day rule you can wait a few dates until you feel comfortable with a person to disclose your status. Yes! I believe you don't have to disclose your status in the beginning when your dating getting to know someone. It's a personal choice to avoid fear or rejection or embarrassment. But if you find yourself in a sexual situation than yes. You must inform the other half your status. You must talk to your sexual partners about your status if you are going to have sex. That goes for both men and women in the heterosexual culture too. Now if you're just dating within the 90 days and you don't see the relationship going anywhere or any further than just friend with benefits status, than have the courage to tell that person straight up your intentions, so they can make the choice on what they want. Knowing your HIV status, telling it to your sexual partner and having them tell you their status before risky behaviors, lessen the chance or getting or transmitting HIV. Sometimes people don't know, are wrong about it, or aren't honest about their status. Depending on the situation, it is a personal choice. If you're not having relations or trying to be in a serious relationship. Then it is a choice to expose your status to someone who's not a doctor at the end of the day. Think about a rejection from a friend, or potential lover may hurt, but a rejection from family our own blood can be extremely painful. Telling people indiscriminately may affect your life in ways you haven't considered. Keep it simple and avoid isolating yourself. You don't have to tell the story of your life. You just want to balance honesty with protecting your right to privacy. Consider the 5 W's. Who do you need to tell? What do you want to tell them about your HIV infection and what are you expecting from the people you are disclosing your HIV status to? When should you tell them? Where is the best place to have this conversation? Why are you telling them?

There is a reason for everything we go through. I've always search for meaning in tragedy or question my reason for the difficulties I had to face in life. I'm not perfect and don't claim to be. I was at one time, looking for love in all the wrong places knowing I wasn't ready yet. It had me struggling with my self-worth. In time as the days gotten worst, I found a way to guard my heart and mind. But I'm no longer in that place or that toxic relationship and now I discovered peace and joy by learning to love, not fear & being single. I love using words to bring hope and healing to others, not as verbal weapons. But to show people that we are all human and we make mistakes. So live life, regardless whether if you are part of a couple. You shouldn't have to wait for another person to feel love or to be able to make moves if your living truthful and living right. If it doesn't work out this is an experience to learn from. I'm just saying don't be afraid to be single. Use the time to develop yourself into the type of person you want to be. Learn who you are without having to rely on another person to complete you.

But remember people come into your life for a reason, season and lifetime. That's life! We face our greatest life challenges when we struggle to find love, security and assurance that life truly has meaning to it. I mean everybody has fears, unhealthy behaviors, and excessive emotional struggles that result from our inability to interpret and correctly cope with our circumstances and feelings. Like I said it's my choice. It's your choice. I understand God wants us to meet a few wrong people before meeting the right one.

So that when we finally meet the right person or our soul mate, we should know how to be grateful to them. No one is perfect when it comes to making life choices. Life does involve making a lot of embarrassing mistakes, meeting people with crazy personality and characteristics probably beyond this world. But if we do come across those negative people in our lives, just try to push them out the way. You do have a choice to be happy. That's my solution to life problems. Anything you've done is totally forgivable, even though it may seem unforgettable to me. Some people can have a negative stronghold on our lives that can hold us back from walking in the fullness of what God has intended for our life and anything that hinders our freedom to do so. But moving forward I have no regrets. It's human nature to go through some break-up agony. I think people need to understand how to cope with and deal with emotions of a breakup. Learning to move on, I know it's sometimes hard to do so. There will be days when things are good and days when you still find yourself wanting to follow the same routine you shared as a couple or when you were dating.

If I could turn back time, I probably would have chosen the path to be single and alone.

Leave it to me to be bold to talk about the past men in my life. I find this to be more of spiritual healing or mental wellness to not only help me but stir up talks on anxiety, fear and stress that I've found we face daily.

So, if you find yourself single like me, don't look at it as a negative thing. Look at it as an opportunity to figure out what truly makes you happy alone with more time and freedom. Remember self-love is a journey. It takes dedications, devotion and practice to love ourselves each day. But when we get it right, watch yourself blossom and your greatest self unfold.

MOVING FORWARD- END NOTES

Be mindful that a request for confidentially is not an absolute guarantee that it will be respected. I realize now that we make the rules. I was a hopeless romantic. And Yes! Love hurts and scars. Love even wounds and marks. But hears the truth now. At one time I shielded my fragile heart. Deep down inside I was not strong enough yet to handle love again. So, I had established rules and set boundaries when it comes to me and love again. But there is an important lesson to learn from solitude and loneliness. Times can be quite tough; they also can show us that our happiness does not have to depend on another person presence. Yet we fear being alone because we assume life is only worth living with another person on our side.

MOVING FORWARD QUESTION.

What is the definition of true love and how do you know when you've found it?

FOUND LOVE- LOST LOVE

Calling all the masses.
Young, Old, Black, White, Gay or Straight.
Together we stand in a world of grace.
But now in this place full of faces of the future.
Crying out in rage, pulsing to the music in my mind standing alone.
Silently beating in your chest to the rhythm of the world's fast pace.
Telling yourself to slow down. You're not ready for love yet.
But I meet what I think is a wonderful guy.

Our bumping and grinding bodies meet.
Blood flowing like the drinks at the bar.
Trying to cover up old wounds, scared by past loves.
Unable to let go of regrets. Bouncing off my emotions.
Unknowing that the secret of my pain is understanding.
That I have found love and lost love.

Oh! Did I mention that I'm going through a rough patch in my life?
Ok! You caught on to the effects of emotions in my voice.
I found myself out trying to forget someone I fell in love with.
Classic bitch behavior. Moving on to the next guy so quickly.
To avoid feeling pain and being alone.

Healing a broken heart can take a while, but it doesn't take forever. It's what I thought.
The pain will past, but it will be difficult to trust and love again.
It sounds like I had too much to drink.
Being pull left and right by friends trying to stand & see through my blurred vision.

You know alcohol can make you have that good feeling with music but have a short-term negative affect on our vision. Head pounding, blood thinning, body being flush out with bottles of water from being too drunk.
Shit! I'll drink to that.

Silently feeling the beat in my chest to the rhythm of the world's fast pace. Telling myself to slow down.
This night out with friends was an eye-opening experience.
A Reality check that made me realize once again that I had found love and lost love. So, I thought.
Or maybe it could have been a great booty call.
Dam! I never got the number, because I was so intoxicated to even ask.

How did I get here? Preaching a sermon called The Healing of Our Damaged Emotions
Most of the people we meet in life aren't meant to stay.
Looking back, it's hard to imagine a better setup for a crash.
I should be focus on what matters and let go of what doesn't.

For now, I'm just a hopeless romantic who found love and lost love. Trying to get over a broken heart.
The agony of loss is baffling experience.
I struggle to resist the temptation to stalk, plead and generally make a needy fool of myself.
Creating a list of reminders to help me become more mindful of my emotions, reframe from urges and set a new course.
But now I see through this haze of pain and understand this method of my sadness.

Together we stand in a world of grace. Young, Old, Black, White, Gay or Straight.
Telling yourself to slow down, to heal from old wounds, scared by past loves.

Look at you, damage goods, a love junkie deprived of a quick fix. Classic bitch behavior from being vulnerable & heart broken.
I understand that you found and lost love. We all have.
But allowing it to mess with your head. Is fuck up!

My goal is to come through this ordeal in one piece and perhaps even emerge better and brighter.
For now, I shall boost my confidence and restore calm by remembering the following.
Always remember the magic of loving you.
When that voice is triggered, I shall turn toward myself or a good friend for reassurance.
I'm Not Crazy!

Chapter Two

RULE #2. Understanding that if you want love, you must apply the 30-60-90 Day Rule, while staying selfless, focus, But not crazy!

How can I be in a relationship? If ultimately, I can't get myself together and focus on a level where my life is balance and focus, even if distractions may appear in our lives. Now before we move on to learn from my mistakes. Have you master the first rule? Are you now ready for love? Because dating itself is already an emotional, confusing whirl wind and then adding on dating rituals and rules like the 30-60-90-day rules is hard itself when looking for love.

If a person goes along with the 30-60-90 Day Rules, it is because they want to invest in a relationship with you. You need time to get to know the person so they will not look at you as hoe, a plaything, or damage goods to be used and discarded. Mindless sex, there's a lot to be said for it. No Commitment, No Disappointments, No Expectations. All one must do is remember your name.

Ok! Let's move forward as we must speak things into existence. The power of the tongue can either be a formidable opponent or your greatest asset. We just need to remember we can own and control both. We ultimately have the power to speak everything into existence. But be careful of what you ask for, if you're not ready it could backfire. But we do want to stay selfless and focus on ourselves and give love a try without losing ourselves. I know it's so hard to do sometimes in this world today, because it's all about skin deep attraction and short-term relationships and the quick fucks which seems to be normal these days. But we have what it takes to make a man or woman fall in love but keeping them from falling out of love is the question. But if you really want to know the truth. A person really want a person that's all the above. Sexy, intelligent, adventurous, quiet and reserve when it's needed. Knowing how to communicate their feelings, to be simple and romantic and cook at home, saving money but also willing to go out and indulge here and there in fine dining and entertainment. These are things that can't be taught, but if you get it right, you just might catch and keep you a man. Keep in mind to do these things when needed and not to smother your mate too much to avoid common pitfalls or breakups. You must provide personal space where both parties can cultivate their personality. One thing I learn from my last breakup. Is when you meet a person? Being honest and trustworthy is key. Helping one another can make life a lot easy. Were all human beings and that's okay. If you fall out of love with a person, I rather you tell me, then lie and carry on in the relationship. Especially within the 90-day rule, because were being seduce with hopes and expectations that a stable relationship will form at the end of the term. At the end of the 90 days or even six months, depending on you. Establish the status of the relationship that you're in. Is it; ***1. Friends with Benefits****, (You both engaging in regular sex, snuggle up together watching tv, hanging out when it feels right?)* ***2. The Place Holder****, (He or She is not looking for a relationship right now. There is no connection or feelings and the relationship is going nowhere. Basically, there waiting around until someone else better comes along.)* ***3. On Going Booty Call****, (You want no relationship with the person other than sex. This can go on for years and emotions can get involved. At some point the romance will passed and you will carry on as casual.)* ***4. Just Talking,*** *(You're flirting through text and in person, nauseating everybody around you or in private, but neither of you will pull the trigger and get official.)* ***5. Sex with an Ex****, (Every now and then, on a drunk evening out, on late night you call your ex and take a cab to their place for some fun. You wake with regret but know full well that you'll probably commit the crime again. After a bottle or two of Pino Noir or heavy alcohol.)* ***6. The App Watch****. (You match with this person on Facebook, Tinder, Adam4Adam or another dating app. You chat every now and then through* *the app's messaging forum, but you have no intentions to meet this person. This person is fun to talk to, but you don't see anything long term happening. Your profile is just giving the impression that your desirable and worth pursuing. But if this status is broken and you meet for sex. Then it's a booty call or one-night stand.)* ***7. One Night Stand****, (You don't really know the person. You slept together one night and fled early that same night or the next morning. But you two must have exchanged phone numbers in a conversion to link u for actions.)* ***8. The Rebound.*** *(You just broke up. Your vulnerable and somebody comes in and sweeps you off your feet or so you think. But these feelings are superficial and that you've unintentionally led this person on. You were in a bad situation and you foolishly embraced whatever good came your way.* ***9. It's Purely Textual****. (You've been texting for weeks/months but haven't met yet. You're interested to some degree, but your just scared to take a just. Be careful on the text language because that could lead you into one of the above status. We have a habit of meeting people online or out, but it leads to nowhere but texting each other what we think we want to here.)* ***10. Just Friends, Who Love Each Other****, (You say you're not dating that your just friends. But your always together and it seems like a couple. Everyone sees it. Stop pretending and make it official. Communicate* *your feelings and make a move.)* ***11. Exclusive****, (Limited to one person and not dating anybody else. There is a period between casual dating and being in a relationship. Getting to know you better, meet your friends, pause your dating apps activity, and agree that you're not seeing anyone else.* ***12. Fast & Furious Side Chick,*** *(I don't condone it, but not everyone can be the starter all the time. And some of you settle into roles as a backup, regardless of their intentions. Some have sex on the first date and then try to leverage that act into love. When you input your feelings of interest and have sex on a first date onto the other person, you often hurt or feel like damage goods, if the other person does not express the same interest or if a second date doesn't evolve. Also avoid those who claims there "not into labels" on relationships after a certain period. This is where you become green, naïve or blind. There the same ones whose probably M.I.A. for major holidays. Who never spends the night? Who always wants to go to your place? Whose probably always on their phone? And you probably will never get to meet his/her friends because you are the side chick? Being in your position can scar you. It can lead you to carry some serious trust issues into future relationships. Just establish the status of the relationship that you're in so you will know where you stand.*

13. Foodie Call Freeloader, *(A new trend where people are sugaring or using dating apps to get free meals, gifts and access to an affluent lifestyle like fine dining and vacations. If you didn't know Sugaring is a form of dating in which a sugar baby goes on dates with a sugar daddy or momma in exchange for something. Basically, a freeloader who cheat people out of love, money or both by going on dates. Even though the relationships are not always sexual in nature.*

But there several good people that want real companionship and are searching for the one or use the dating as a source of enjoyment that helps establish self and social confidence. Dating can be fun and a great healthy social interaction and can be a learning experience when both sides haves a positive attitude to making their date interesting. At worst, some use the ample opportunity of meeting people through dating apps for no good. But how can we stop this. That's easy. Don't go out for dinner quickly after matching on an app or even if you meet them out on the streets. Start with something small like; a hike, a picnic, a walk or free coffee or water you bring for conversation in a public place. Do whatever you need to do to avoid the side hustle of a freeloader.

If you made it. Congratulations the screening process is over, you pass the trial period and became a full-time hire.

Just remember you can be more than one status types at a time. But if you did make it to exclusive type, congratulations. You're no longer hooking up with other people and you're essentially only emotionally invested in one another. Your slowing ready or steady moving in together. Working toward goals for longevity and a commitment to working things out when problems arise. Because a relationship is an investment in the future and is not something that should be assumed.) People need to understand that breaking someone heart is going to be more painful than standing in the relationship with a lie. Their world will be upside down for minute and you probably send them into an emotional spin fueled by fear, sadness, and anxiety. But that's OK! That's why we have counseling and/or our circle of close friends to help us through. And if you don't, behind closed doors we talk to ourselves and God about inconsequential things to get us through hard times. Epiphany! Why is it that our best friends have become part of our lives long before we went on a catch a man and keep him campaign? If we could only just stay single and just stick with our principles and values. Do you think the right guy would came along and give us a chance at real love if we've waited? I'm so tired of being disappointed, that I'm encouraging everyone who's ever been heartbroken to join me on this campaign movement on protecting yourself. Shit protecting your heart. Learn from my mistake if not any. Let me tell you. I tried to put myself back out there too fast, not thinking about the 30-60-90-day rule and how to use it to maneuver my dating life. Having one-night stands. I was having trouble distinguishing the difference between love vs passion and lust. Think about it? We all know that one-night stands are one of the worse ways to meet and fall in love. Question? Could you love someone, who would share their whole being with you, after only knowing you for hours? Can having sex with a man too soon be the fastest way to drive him away instead of bringing him closer? So many questions racing through my mind and so few answers to them. Why would we put ourselves out there to go through all that? What is it that makes us want someone who does not want us back? Exploration for true love, we all hope to find. It is one step closer to the truth and meaning we've been searching for in our life's. Now let's take a look at the 30-60-90 Day rules.

The 30-Day Rule. *Look I do believe that dating multiple people is a choice. Within the first 15 minutes you meet someone, I know that I have a physical attraction. This initial attraction stirs up neurotransmitters and hormones that create the excitement of infatuation and a strong desire to be* *close and sexual with a person. That's not love. These chemicals and our emotions and psychological makeup can cause us to be with him or her. Actions speaks louder than words isn't just a cliché. When it's purely lust, were not too interested in spending time together without sex or the expectation of it. The truth is you can be completely be ignorant to the fact that one person has develop feelings for someone that could maybe be there hormones creating this strong desire of lust. But can they last 30 Days to capture my soul & mind with rich deep stimulating, intellectual, spiritual conversation. And in return I reward you with the same and a few kisses but no sex. Relationships that start off with sex to soon always end bad. No one appreciates anything they can get easy and free. So, I suggest that you wait 30 Days. Anyone can put on a façade, fake it, make themselves look way better than they are, but not many can stretch that out over a month or two. The truth comes out in the wash and it takes a little time for the wash to come completely clean. Also, you find out if the guy is really truly interested in you or if he is just looking for a quick fuck. If he is just looking for a no strings-attached sex, he won't wait it out. He will just move on to another person that will put out immediately. If they really like you, they will get to know you. And if it is real it will be the same in 30 days or 30 dates but nevertheless you be able to tell what his true intentions are. Trust me when you have those who say they don't play mind game's; they always have a hidden agenda. They be the same ones who toy with your emotion, who's not interested in you, but want to fuck you on the first night or within 30 days of you meeting. They pretend with excuses when it comes time to commit. Those are the same head strong, too aggressive, too demanding, too materialistic, controlling people who have stubborn personality traits that refuse to change their opinions about a situation. Which is due to a lack of influence or knowledge in their community or there just covering up controlling behaviors. If you say that you want to be in a relationship but is consistently unavailable to get it together with you. Why don't they communicate that? Say that you're not able to focus and commit to trying to pursue a relationship. And if you just want to Netflix and chill and just fuck with no strings attach. Shit! Just let me know upfront. So, I can make the choice or not, if that's something I want to do. At the end of the day. They treat you like an option. They call you up when they want something. It might be money, attention, an ego stroke, sex, an armchair psychologist, but if you think back to all the times when you've heard from them, you may notice that it was a preamble to something.*

The 60 Day Rule. *This is where some of you fail. The 60 Day No Contact Rule. Remember in the beginning when your single & mingling you can date multiple people without sex. But now that we have chosen our candidate and made it past the 30 Days to the 60 Day mark. The no contact rule means you basically cut off all communication with everyone else i.e.; exes for a certain amount of time. Some would say another 30 days is enough, but 60 days is better. Every relationship is different. This no contact rule allows you to cool down, process your feelings and think rationally about the real reasons you're not together anymore with exes, while you are talking to someone else. This new relationship must be defined, which is the most awkward thing to do when navigating in a new relationship. You want to be sure if this is a new friendship, a casual hookup or are you two exclusive. Which you will learn more about that in my closure rule. But, right now you're still dating and in the 60-day mark and it's still not time to make a commitment yet. Enjoy all the flowers and lovely dates and long talks. Spend time together doing as many different things as you can think of. Think of different endearing ways to admire and appreciate each other but don't say I love you, don't move in together, and don't make any long-term commitments. Your hormones are still in control and they have no agenda* *except to mate. Remember sometimes we find our special lover and it can last a lifetime. We usually fall in love several times, so we have, to have a plan of action that will keep yourself safe when you start falling in love again.*

This is the time to just relax and enjoy the process. Don't expect to marry every single person you date. Plan to just enjoy the date and the person company and to be your best self on the dates and expect that there's a 50-50 chance that it works out or not. So, focus less on your mental checklist and more on how the other person makes you feel. Through this experience, both of you, whether you're attracted to each other or not, will learn something if you're open to it. Maybe you have a good time and realize what you don't want in someone. Maybe you find a friend who will pay a hug role in your life. Or maybe you will never see this person again. But with this mindset, it doesn't matter. Its more about the opportunity to experience a new person and hopefully learn something about yourself.

The 90-Day Rule. *So, you waited 90 days, had a few dates, a little fun, a few kisses and even got to know him or her. Do you like the person? Can you see a future together? Have you been approaching dating as your authentic, honest self? Have you turn your dial from "Finding the One" to "Getting to Know Somebody"? Have you gotten rid of your checklist* *and focus on how someone makes you feel and the ability they must create a sense of space in your life? How many times did your intuition kicked in when you avoided sex from being in the heat of passion? Was he able to withstand, withhold and avoid having sex with other past encounters? Sometimes our intuition or six sense will give us signs that the person we are pursuing is unfaithful and have not let their other past encounters go during the 60-Day rule like you did. But no need to put pressure on the person and the sex part of starting a relationship. In other words, it's best to wait at least until you're comfortable with each other and have a better picture of what each person wants in the relationship. But when it comes to how much time it takes, it depends. It could be a few weeks, a few months or until you get married.*

As the future stretches out in front of us like a desolated desert. Were unable to control our feelings. It's like losing everything. The loss of hope. And knowing that life would never feel so good again without it. I kelp asking for love to come into my life so many times, even when I was not ready for it. Knowing that I was on a personal journey to heal and to reestablish balance back in my life.

I don't know. I'm tired of never knowing. No one knows what the outcome ever is. What a person is thinking. But for some reason it leaves an empty space in our hearts that were all trying to fill. We can't help but to keep trying to put ourselves out there. Hoping life will ever feel so good again someday with a companion to share it with. I know what you are thinking. Is he crazy having sex too early with a man he barely know? Especially if he's looking. Clearly, it's the reason why men pull back after having sex too soon. Which is part of what makes our situation in trying to find another male companion complicated. We don't apply the 90-day rule when dating or meeting a person. Sometimes men think different about sex. Because were men, we fall into our own trap when it comes to looking for a relationship. Doubting ourselves, asking questions like women? No! I'm not labeling women as weak. I just don't want to be label as a hoe or even carry this type of label around near a man that I'm seriously trying to get to know or interested in. How do I know if this guy will pursue a relationship with me and not be focused just on casual sex? I cannot get caught up in a trap with a man like this. It will be very hard to escape a relationship like this if my feelings get involve. And let's not forget stress due to the lack of commitment. Things like this could emotionally weaken you and lead to long term stress arising from incomplete and non-satisfactory emotional fulfillment. Some would argue I should be patient, and that love will find me.

That's what I had to tell myself. That it was just an interaction between two people who are looking to get to know one another better, with or without commitments or promises. Don't get me wrong, this is only just the first night and sometimes relationship do blossom within one-night stands. But I think what I need to do is learn to distinguish the difference between love vs. passion and lust. I do believe we should throw ourselves out there to experience both ups and down. I'm not saying go out and be a slut and sleep with every man you can grab because you feel like it. But take a risk, experiment to find real love. This is and will be preparation for the heart to be ready for when real love or Mr. Right comes along. So, one-night stand or not I guess I'll find out. I just hope I remember this every time I put myself back and forth out there.

Epiphany! There was red flags that I didn't catch on to, until I had those experiences. I had discovered flaws about myself that had me feeling and living wrong. The thought of my pain and me being hopeless is a bitter poison. I think of it constantly, and my spirit is depressed. When your world is falling apart, it's so easy to focus on the pain, the problems, the pressure and the difficulties. It's the natural response. I was mad at the world. Change my thoughts. Faith in the unchangeable character of God is the only bedrock upon which a person's spiritual life can be founded. I understand if you want love, you must speak love while staying selfless, focus, but not crazy. I must believe and not slack in my quest for a deeper spiritual experience. I understand there will be distraction in my life, that's why I welcome any manifestation of the spirit of God in my life and not proudly assume I don't need it, but if God decides not to use me to prop up others and my spiritual life, it merely proves the depth of his confidence in me. He obviously believing I have the grit to tough it out by raw faith.

But hey! I'm just one man and there is no instructions manual for relationships, no rules set in stone, but rather theories or opinions that people believe work. But I do believe we need the discipline to wait 90 days. To be honest, having sex with a guy during the first 30 days is risky territory. Consider this the no expectation period. The 60 days should be the time where both of you are romancing each other. And to decide whether you want to keep him around for love, sex or nothing at all. I believe the 90-day Rule is designed to help you take the time to get to know someone until you trust that they have a good intentions towards you. In fact, you may not necessarily feel comfortable with them yet and they must respect your wishes or move on without you. But make sure you communicate your goals with them to make sure you're on the same page. Because they may not be able to commit to only you during this period. In fact, you don't necessarily have to commit to him during this period, either. We should be using the 90 days to explore the dating world, so you don't have to put your eggs all in one basket.

MOVING FROWARD- END NOTES

Something people need to know. Causal sex is not a way to cure a broken heart. Love is an over-powering feeling, when we fall for someone, you fall fast. But it's a struggle we must endure alone and lesson we need to learn, in order to figure things out. I remember so many rejections. Too many blows to heart. There's so much a person can endure before its starts to take a toll. I say trust no one for the moment. Guard what's most precious to you. And that is your heart. Or this pattern of being heartbroken will repeat itself repeatedly. So, let's explore the ins and outs of the 30-60-90-day rule, and how you can use it to maneuver your dating life.

MOVING FORWARD QUESTIONS.

What goals are important for any couple to conquer as they progress throughout life?

THE TRUTH POTION #9

My garden of potions is like a paradise so let me take you out of this world and into total ecstasy.
This spell that breaks all barriers, love, success, health and more.
In order to speak truth, you must first feel confidant and secure in who you are.

Ask yourself what are you truly capable of?
In order to accept yourself, you need to know yourself.
Why do you fear being alone?
Why is it that when your heart's broken, you cry for days, maybe weeks?
Rejection is nothing. It has no impact on you unless you let it have an impact on you.

Truth is; the only way you are going to be valued and respected. Is to stand up for yourself.
At the end of the day, this is all that matters.

Love can change your world, but should you let it change who you are as a person?
What can you do to gain your confidence back?
Transform your appearance.
Changing everything from the hairstyle, teeth and clothing, to your posture and voice.
If it makes you feel more confident, I guess.
But do it for you. Do it with a smile on your face?
Changing or trying to change who you are will spell nothing but trouble if the change isn't authentic and natural.
Shit! I've notice it is what been alter, is what people view about you anyways. Good or Bad.
It's often isn't until we meet someone that we start to realize that we need to look after ourselves.

It happens to everyone eventually.

Something deeply ratter your confidence.
I'm not saying compare yourself to others.
But there is a hidden Gem of learning here.
If we want to give out our best, exercise more or eat a better diet. Be the person you want to become.

We all have that seductive and alluring beauty.
You just need to sharpen your image to have a polished appearance.

Let's see, the question is now?
Can you create a confident appearance?
Do you have the power to allure?
That magical power to attract.
Can you slip into your silkiness and your sensuality?
Or shall I conjure up this this lie of witch's brew and call it Love Potion #9. My Truth Potion.

Can you transform yourself the natural way and learn what makes a person attractive to you?
Hint! It begins with attractive qualities in which you can control and change about yourself.
Intelligence, Confidence, Being Sweet and thoughtful.
Shit! Try to look good, but you don't really have to alter your appearance surgically?
You possess the power and have the capacity to use it to produce desirable results.
I'm just here to help you develop this formula and add my ingredients of developing courage and self-confidence to your life in your own unique way of course.

Sexual attraction weave stories of bliss when its reciprocated, but what happens when It's not.

No Fat, No Femmes, No Asians, No Blacks is disgustingly frequent mantra and yet it is racist.
But you can't get made if the person doesn't want you.
If you get rejected, brush it off and keep it moving on.
That's the true formula here.
Confidence. Being true and authentic.
Trusting yourself to make the right choices.
That's the true formula here.

Being confident doesn't mean that you are never afraid.
If doesn't mean you have life figured out and you know exactly what you are doing at any given moment.
Being confident is about trusting yourself and knowing that you will be ok whatever that path may take you.
Your confidence is at the core of everything that your either attracting or repelling in your life.
It makes all the difference in the type of relationship you attract or don't attract.
And the potential partners who find you or avoid you.

The question is are you committed to creating and sustaining a great level of confidence and a relationship with yourself.
That is the true potion.

Chapter Three

Rule#3. The Magic Formula: Use the 3 F's (Fashion, Fun, Flirt) for attention, being desirable & mysterious to keep a person interested

Let's talk about the secret formula of confidence. There is a formula for being desirable and mysterious to keep a person interested. That's my love Potion mix with the truth to bring out your confidence. But most people have trouble creating mystery and intrigue in their intimate relationship or when dating. Sometimes we get too comfortable, too familiar and feel that the other person no longer excites them. Most people have low standards and low self-steam for themselves and so they let everything go, believing that since they've been with the person for a while, they feel accepted and loved for who they are. Ok! Well you keep believing that.

Let's face it image is an issue for many men, regardless of sexuality. Just because you been with a person for a while or even living single, you feel as if your accepted & love doesn't mean you should lower your standards. A lot of women and my gay friends say they struggle to find any sort of meaning relationship because people are so focus on physicality and nothing else. Yes! It is so superficial and it's sad. But everyone has something beautiful about them and we shouldn't be looking at the body.

But our attractions and fetishes are cultural phenomena; they are a product of our surroundings. Images of perfect bodies are everywhere in gay culture. Even the way we look for potential partners is tainted by this; the gay app technology our generation has grown up with necessitates that we use a profile picture to identify if they'd be a good date, or a lay. Look at the gay community for instants. We categorize men by body type (twinks, bears, otters, etc.) and use the system to filter out who we potentially find attractive. This strict categorization usually idealizes masculinity and it is easy for many of us to fall through the cracks. Thin boys are designated as twinkies, too femme for many to fuck, and the bear tribe requires a very specific amount of fat, muscle and fur. To be fat in a thin-obsessed gay culture can be difficult. Despite affectionate in-group monikers for big gay men, chubs, bears, cubs, the anti-fat stigma that persists in American culture which still haunts individuals who often exist at the margins of gay communities. 'No fats, No Femmes, No Asians, No Blacks' is a disgustingly frequent mantra on a gay app and the scariest part is there are a huge swathe of today's generation of gay men who are too dense to realize that this is not only deeply racist or prejudice, but thinks it natural. It' s not just gay men, its women too. You're taste in men, your fetishes, your attitudes towards dating are all products of the society that you grew up in. Not all men are like this. It is such a deep-rooted problem that there is no immediate solution to it. Maybe considering that there might be a problem within our culture as gay men or any culture, would be a step towards just talking more about a solution. A solution on combating being complacent and how people are uncomfortable with the understanding and seeing body image, gender, sexual satisfaction and relationship qualities, because of what it affords them or how they view themselves and each other as they interact in important ways like relationship satisfaction or sexual satisfaction. But then again love, desire and sexual attraction weave stories of bliss when they're reciprocated, but what happens when they're not? As much as we may wish it to be otherwise so, some people may not want them; as date, a boyfriend, a partner, a wife and a husband. What do we do when the person we want doesn't want us back? These moments of unreturned love or lust may be tough. They may feel gut-wrenching sad, confusing, bare, lonely and vulnerable. And yet they are tough reality and togetherness and separateness. Sometimes the person you most want doesn't want you or to play your game. We can't control what people decide to do with their lives. Not only can we not control it but sometimes the kindest, most compassionate response is to acknowledge that whatever the other person chose is perhaps best for them now. Maybe there not trying to be cruel by hurting your feelings. There's no doubt about it: unrequited love and lust are hard. But know your worth, you can't get mad. We must continue to move forward in pursuit of exploring the scene until the right one comes along that finds us attracted back.

Now Fashion, Fun, Flirt can drive people to attempt to achieve an unattainable ideal. It is what's inside that is most important. But there's nothing wrong with wanting to look your best, it's just when you become so obsessed with how you look that you waste an enormous amount of time, energy, money and resources. You spend too much time looking good, means you have less time to be good. I find a person mysterious and fascinating when there real and show their true selves. I see their true natural beauty. That's what I'm drawn and attracted too. I feel like I'm connected to them and that they see the world exactly the way I do. And that's mysterious to me, even if they do not make some what a conscious effort to be mysterious. But we are meant to be mysterious in our own way and fascinating to people when we come across them. We attract, produce fire and create intense sexual energy because they're different and real and that these energies were giving off are meant to feed one another. You can be mysterious simply by embodying your true self. Anyone who is authentic, confident, and real, has self-respect and tends to be unique is mysterious naturally to me.

That's the advantage here to the game. Knowing how to flirt and be mysterious and desirable to get a person interested and then taking the next steps to keep them interest or to even have fun and live a little. Yet we can't help but to get caught up in the mix of our own feelings." We are not perfect, but we are perfect in knowing that we are not perfect." Falling for ever pretty thing that cross our paths. Subjectivity are influences, informs, and biases that affect people's judgements about truth or reality. I find myself drawn to the wrong people all the time. Wanting to know more because of their looks. And it is here when we get caught up in the mix of our own game of love. Sometimes not being ready, having open the window likely to be a victim running around like a chicken with my head cut off, letting the current take my feelings wherever it wants to take me.

Fashion: *Let's take a closer look at how fashion is important and how people define themselves and how it* *affect our dating prospects. I believe it's just a psychological thing that affects people insecurities regarding the way they look in regards to fashion choices. This can affect both your self-image, the impression that conveyed to others and in turn, the way in which people behave towards you. In many societies, your dress sense embodies personal wealth and taste. Which has an influence on our species in evolutionary. Psychologist suggests that our behavior is determine by our efforts to find a mate and to reproduce. It's ashamed clothes matter and the wardrobe says a lot about you. Let's use this rule to try to wheel out conceited people who idolize themselves. Vanity is defined as excessive pride and an over estimation of one's merit and abilities. Those who make their clothes a principal part of themselves, will in general become of no more value than their clothes.*

Fun: *What we should be focusing on is making dating fun and less stressful. Which resolves around your mindset going in. We put way too much pressure on love. Dates are meant to be fun activities. If you are looking for love, don't make it about being desired. But instead let's get out and do something we want to do. Don't make the date about carrying their approval or desire. Remember that your date needs to fit comfortably into your life. Instead of getting* *caught up in wanting to be desired, take a mental step back and ask yourself if you even like the version sitting across from you. If your too caught up in seeking validation, your likely to be disingenuous and create a superficial connection. So instead of putting on a perfect persona, cut the stress out an enjoy your story and share some of your own. It don't have to be an interview. Depends on how well the date is going, you must have a concrete plan that takes stress out of dating, so take it a step further. Consider upgrading and down grading your dates at any time, so if you're not vibing with the person, promise to cut them and your time off after the first drink. Cut ties, move on, and never look back. There is no rule to say that you must stick it out. Your free to be (or not be) with whomever you choose. Just be honest and open about it to avoid wasting your time. When you meet the right one and fall in love, it will cancel out every other person who didn't matter from the start. That's something I really want, and you want to deep down inside.*

Of course, we all want to find real love. But life is a game in which we can't control. But making bad decisions in life will lead you to fall in love with the wrong person simply because the wrong guy usually looks good and says all the right things. Love is blind? Does it blind you from the truth? Yes, it can. Let me tell you. I fell victim to my own rules. Trying to get to know someone base on looks and ended up getting cheat on. Deep down I already know the answers to my own question. Why! I just didn't want to believe it. When you love someone there is a certain amount of denial that is built into facing the fact that they would betray you in such a way. Cheating is very hard & painful to go through. A lot of people rather deny it, then face truth at the end of their relationship. Love is not blind. People choose to turn a blind eye to certain situations because they don't want to lose that feeling, that dream of love.

***Flirting**: There's an art of exclusive flirting. In other words, if he or she uses casual flirting vs true affection, there probably nothing more behind it. Flirtation is a way to feel you out before putting yourself on the line. And if you know the difference between flirting and love, you can avoid getting hurt. If you're interested in someone romantically, you might flirt with them. Which means to chat them up or tease in a playful way. Flirting is an indirect and fun way to let your crush or partner know that you're interested in them. Think of Love as a full glass of milk. Flirting is like adding too much sugar, which heighten the taste to be too sweet to drink. It might be good* *for some to drink but not all. But just remember flirting is a big part of dating. And you don't want a person to misinterpret your motives.*

Although we know the formula for being desirable and mysterious to keep a person interested. Now it's all about knowing how to manage the difference between lust and love. There's nothing wrong with flirting, but don't confuse flirting vs true attraction. It will have you wrapped up confuse with sex or lust with love. Lust, sometimes seen as the power that drives modern love, it has worn away over time. Lust in some relationships recedes, and with that the relationship typically ends. Is it right to assume that those relationships that continue lust after said chemicals dissipate, are that of true romantic love? "I had thought at times that I had known love, but in hindsight I can tell that it was simply being attractive & lust that attracted me to the idea of spending the rest of my life with a person. I look back, and I now know the difference to my situation is that of a flashlight compared to the sun. I had a chance to examine a bad relationship that continue lustful. And I see that the definition of unstoppable true romantic love seems to be prevalent among even today's questioning society.

True intimacy cannot exist when you build walls of lies around each other. It's funny when I hear those words. To me honesty and trust are vital to the success of a relationship. Keeping secrets only create problems. A question for my reader? Are you ready to be in a relationship? I had used this Love Potion #9 to get this man I found very attractive. But now, what do you do when the feeling and thrill wears off and the more you have sex or do anything, the less you like it? Can't you see he or she is not the one? Do you believe that what we really want is not sex, but true intimacy? Do we stay in a relationship where there's nothing but lies and deception? Although we both were attracted to each other, neither one of us was ready for a relationship. Our signs got cross in flirting.

But let's end this on a good note. We know now that the secret formula is confidence. Sometimes we get too comfortable and we jump into relationships when were not ready. As a confident person we analyze everything, to see if a person really like us, because we assume, they do. People with high self-esteem believe they are worthy of love and don't question how someone feels about them, because they know they are good, competent and lovable and trust that the right person for them will see this. To me I don't care if you're a confident person or have low self-esteem. No one should have to feel stressed and anxious when a person feeling is unclear. We assume that a person like us when they make it known, but we want to enjoy that person without being weighed down by problems, fears and doubts. One thing I won't do is stress when it comes to dating & relationships. I'm not perfect, but I do love myself no matter what.

EVOLUTION

Where is evolution taking us?
I would like to know will our descendants hurtle through space as relatively unchanged humans like the ones in the movie on a starship enterprise.
Because your president, not mines, mention space force.

Will they be muscle bound cyborgs?
Or will they close to digitize their consciousness's becoming electronics immortals?

We in danger girl.
The same way our little robots struggle to survive against the unknown universe, so do we all.

Stay with me people, I'm stepping outside the box for a moment.
I would like to know the evolution on our sex lives.

Why is sex so important?
As we evolved as humans, so do our connections for love changes over time in our relationships.
But because we have evolved, but it is natural to imagine if we can do more.

In fact, welcome to your sex life.
Where the basis has change.
How do we evolve the most loving brain on the planet?

People are always pouring out their hearts and soul to others.
And some decipher that as being a freak or sex addict.
Sexual compatibility is much more significant in the well-being of a relationship than its given credit for.
To make sense of it. I have evolved to the next level.

At this point in our human history we can map it out in stages.
One, our love relationship and sexual selection process is driven by basic instants; food, shelter and sex.

At the next level, a deep sense of magical belonging to a partner emerges. Someone who makes us feel like were the most important people in the world.

Next, we desire a partner who satisfies our ego by giving us all that we ever wanted and deserved right now.

As we evolve further, we realize that sexual, magical and romantic feelings do not equate love, which leads to immense guilt when we try to separate.
Last, we seek a new partner when the existing partner can no longer support us in reaching our goals.

Finding a sexually compatible partner is complicated by other factors as well.
Especially for the gay community. Stigma and shame mean people are not always comfortable disclosing their sexual interests or level of desire.

Dear Society, Heartbroken Black Men need love too.
Their feelings and mix emotions are no longer there.
Until we show young black boys that their manhood can and should include organically navigating the range of human emotions, were going to continue to cultivate Black Men who know nothing about coping, managing, or evening accepting their natural feelings.
Express your desires.
Give your partner the opportunity to meet your needs.
There is much more evolution that goes into the naughty aspects of sex.

I have discovered my deepest and inner sexiest secrets hidden within me.
Only to not attract the right person just like me.
Translation: Your Best friend, your lover, your sunshine, your everything.
The choices of choosing a mate with mental traits have evolve therefore having a stronger sexual selection.

All things must evolve.
Intimacy! Be vulnerable & Entrust yourself to allow a person to see who you really are.
Because If everything around you has been the same, It's time for drastic change.
Mutual respect, love and understanding bonds us together into a deeper understanding.
For some change can lead to confusion.
Buts it's a common misunderstanding that evolution has not taken place for you yet.

Chapter Four

Rule#4. The New Sex Rule. Time Change, and the gender roles we play by in the bedroom change right along with them.

Have you notice people sex drive has change? Maybe an individual's strong urge for sex can help identify that he or she may be more likely to cheat. After all, we know that different people crave sex to different degrees. And those of us who have exceptionally strong sex drives are more likely to be unfaithful. Therefore, we must go back to rule 1. Learning self-love and self-control first. Which refers to the ability to regulate impulse, such as caving into a temptation if it's not monogamous with your partner. Think, Self-control can be look at like a muscle and as a muscle, it might become tired when overused. But just remember neither self-control nor sexual desires are the only factors involving in predicting infidelity. At the end of the day, you must communicate your needs to each other. Many men/women have trouble being assertive. Probably because they shy away from conflict and don't want to trouble or inconvenience the other. They constantly let other people needs supersede their own and they find it difficult to articulate their personal goals and desires. No one's a mind reader. You can't intuitively know what someone need without having to say anything. So, ask and communicate things you need in the relationship. You are the expert on your own body and mind.

Putting your secret desires out there can be scary no matter how close you are to your partner. Once you're comfortable discussing your turn-ons through other people's fantasies, then you can begin to explore your own. If you don't feel comfortable describing your fantasies, try talking about sexy sensations: the feel of his strong hands on your body, his warm breath on your neck, the enveloping mild breeze on a walk through the park that made you feel relaxed and sensual. Healthy communication is one of the most important parts of a relationship. Even if you're just talking about how your day went, that is something. Try to spend more time together. Find out more about him or her; what are their dreams are, their passions, their deepest desires, etc.? This kind of conversation fosters intimacy and it will make your relationship a lot stronger. Try something new together. Being adventurous isn't all about having sex in adventurous ways. You and your honey can improve your relationship by stepping out of your comfort zones and trying something wild and new together.

Kinky is the new way. It's all about being open an trying new things beyond what you been doing. I never thought of myself as kinky. It is a confusing term. Where, exactly is the line drawn. What's makes anyone "kinky" rather than just open or adventurous? The kinky expansion of sexual possibilities comes with the great advantage of being able to make up your own relationship rules. This is fun, because you can completely come up with your own framework. But the downside of this is that you must establish these rules with each other, not just yourself. Who said we must follow what society has set for us? "How do I handle my relationship in such a way, that my kink becomes an expansion of my repertoire rather than a source of unhappiness. How do I keep relationship rules in harmony with what my heart wants? How do I prevent myself from not fixating on just one sides of the "rules"? When it comes to sex, you've probably already figured out that what works for one couple doesn't always work for another. Yet even as we write our own unique sex scripts, a lot of us end up following some old-fashioned rules in bed anyways.

Sharing the most intimate details of your sex life is still largely taboo. Now I don't recommend sharing and exploring your sexual desires during the beginning dating stages. The truth is that at least some of your friends have probably tried it and one out of five make it part of their regular play in the bedroom. Keep in mind your grown ass adults and can do whatever with your life. For those who are not sure of the kinky sex umbrella. Try low-risk activities. You don't want to find yourself in a situation where you want to knowingly engage in high-risk sex. Put your safety first. Your safe sex practices can be compromised and less effective if you misread the signs from you partner. The use of condoms is not negotiable for you? Every day you find it more difficult to find partners like you who like safe sex.

It's no surprise that since we don't talk about kinky sex, there are a lot of myths and misconceptions floating around. Let's clear the air on a few common kink stereotypes. Keeping bedroom play fun and safe can have a lot of benefits, and even though it can be whatever you and your partner want it to be, there are still a few things you should keep in mind so that your explorations are fun, safe, and positive. Exploring kink doesn't have to begin with buying a leather body suit and a whip. It can be as simple as seeing what happens when you break from your regular bedroom routine and enter a new world of sex. The core tenets of successful kinky sex are like those of any strong, long-term relationship: communication, trust, understanding and patience. But what exactly qualifies as kinky? Let's look at a few things. ***1. BDSM.*** *When most people think of kinky sex, they think of BDSM, a four-letter acronym that stands for six different things: Bondage, Discipline, Dominance, Submission, Sadism, and Masochism. BDSM includes an extremely wide range of activities, from light paddle spanking and dominant/submissive role-playing to bondage parties and pain play.* ***2. Fantasy and role-playing.*** *One of the most common forms of kinky sex involves creating imagined scenarios. This could be as simple as talking about a fantasy in bed, to as complex as wearing costumes or acting out scenes in front of strangers.* ***3. Fetishes.*** *One out of four men and women are interested in fetish play, defined as treating a nonsexual object or body part sexually. Common fetishes include the feet and shoes, leather or rubber, and diaper play.* ***4. Voyeurism or exhibitionism.*** *Watching someone undress or watching a couple have sex without their knowledge are common voyeur fantasies, while having sex in a public place is one form of exhibitionism.* ***5. Group sex.*** *Threesomes, sex parties, orgies, and more. Group sex is any act that* *involves more than two people. "Kink" itself might refer to anything that bends away from the straight and narrow. But at the end of the day just make sure that the relationship is mutually monogamous, which means you are both committed to only having sex with each other and trusting that there open and honest about your sexual activity past and present. It's also important to note that people's actual sexual behaviors are constrained, in part, by their partner's sexual preference. There are no absolutes when it comes to an individual's sexual preference. Some men just don't fit into "traditional" sexual and gender roles in the gay society. Some men use these terms as a guide, while others see them as a necessary protocol to follow. Either way, it's an important conversation to have before sex or dating. If we all can just live in our truth without fear and discrimination. It's bad enough people are scared to come out because the risks of meeting prejudice and discrimination.*

There is an importance to your satisfaction. Especially sexual compatibility, compatibility of turn on and turn offs. This is just one of the aspects of relationship to concentrate on. Human beings need sex, sex is essential for our physical happiness. When you're not fulfilled by each other sexual needs and desires, dissatisfaction in the relationship is quite the obvious result. But society has made sex into a taboo sport and people find attributing sexual incompatibility as a reason to break up.

How would you feel if it turned out that the reason why that people break up with you, had nothing to do with when you chose to sleep with them? To tell you the truth, there wasn't enough chemistry or potential compatibility to move forward. But that doesn't mean that sex was all he or she wanted from the get-go. Having different level of sex drives and the desire to have sex could be an issue as well. But let's face it. They were basically scared to communicate and admit that you two had no future together. Listen time has change and any of the rules and guidelines that have been drilled into our heads have been distorted. Consider this other possibility. You could have done everything right and waited several dates to have sex and he still could have done a post-coital bail. Maybe that's how it was going to play out all along.

As we all get older with time, our appearance changes, our interests change, and even the way we conduct ourselves in relationship to others change. Big changes represent a direct contradiction to your own thoughts or values, which is what makes them so difficult to swallow. Let's move forward when it comes to sex, and the new sex rule. Let's make our own rules. In time people will discover I hope what works for one couple, doesn't always work for another. I think when it comes to the sex rules, the only rule it should be, is that you and your partner must be open for change. There are only deep emotions two people get when making love. Love is more than emotions and it is much more than a good feeling too. The kind of sex life you and your partner have, and its conflict are embedded in the overall relationship you learn and practice of with your partner.

I believe that the information I will give you, will put you in the right direction of understanding men and women but also the sex roles have evolved, but are kind of similar on both sides gay or straight. Time has change. People are craving sex more, not relationships. This is where we encourage people to have open discussions about such issues that will help set boundaries and hopefully avoids hurt feelings down the line. Some of us have a dark kinky side to us. But keep your private life private. It's nobody business but our own of what goes on in the bedroom. I know what I want and what I like. I settle for nothing less and ask the same of in return from any companion I may meet.

I leave you with this, stay safe. It always been my agenda to promote awareness and equal rights and safe sex. And if that takes talking about sex to reach a lot uneducated people then so be it. I believe gay couples should have the same rights as straight couples. Talking about it and pushing this agenda is an important step on the path to equality and freedom for all Americans. Even though we all make mistakes, just wrap it.

MOVING FORWARD- END NOTES

In human sexuality, Top. Bottom and Versatile are sex positions during sexual activity, especially between two men. But its time to stop pigeonholing gay men as tops and bottoms. Ultimately, if you're looking for love it's the person, not their sexual role that you're going to connect with. That is what holding a lot of people back from meeting a perfect mate.

MOVING FORWARD- END NOTES

It's our choice to choose an undeniable relationship between sex and love. With all these variables it's unlikely that the relationship between love and sex will ever be a simple or static one.

MOVING FORWARD: END NOTES

Sometimes we live in a world of fantasy.
Escapism from all problems.
But sometimes you must leave your fantasy world and live out loud.
The desire to have another person is an unhealthy way of coping with the challenges of life.
So, stop withdrawing from the pressure of the real world and living into a safer fantasy world.
Because we are ultimately responsible for all the decisions that we make and actions that we take.

HOPELESS ROMATIC

Long days.
Short nights.
Pain hurts.
And remembering what hurts more.
Decision made affecting the future made in the past.
Affect the heart of a young lover scorn.
Falling in love never hurt anybody, so they say.
But living the lifestyle of a hopeless romantic.
Wearing your heart on your sleeve.
Looking, praying, wishing love would find me, but it never does.
Having so much love to give, but no one to share it with.
Hurts more than being alone.
The faces we wear, hiding our real emotions from the world we live in.
This truly affects us physically, emotionally and mentally.
People not understanding that the decisions (They/ We) make.
Affect someone other than ourselves.

Chapter Five

Rule#5. The Conscious Rethink Rule. Follow your deepest inner intuition and knowing. This will help guide you in making choices on dating & sleeping with the wrong person.

At some point you will realize that you have done too much for someone, that the only next possible step to do is to just stop. Leave them alone and walk away. It's not like you're giving up, and its not like you shouldn't try. Its just that you must draw the line of determination from desperation. What is truly yours will eventually be yours and what is not, no matter how hard you try, will never be.

Ask yourself this? Is he or she right for me? How do I tell if they aren't? The truth is; they will express it. Being deeply loved by someone gives you strength and courage. And you will see the undeniable signs that a person is really in love with you. So, don't try to change him or her, they will change themselves if they love you.

It's all about chemistry, sharing common values and interest, how you communicate, how he/she makes you feel and whether he/she treats you with respect. Once you determine your priorities and evaluate your relationship and communicate it together, it's time to conscious rethink if the person is right for you. Finding the right one is not easy for most of us. If you have not found the one that is for you, don't fret. Instead of looking at other people's flaws, focus on constantly improving yourself first.

Listen have you ever been into a relationship where you doubted if you made the right decision by committing into a relationship with a guy who, it turns out, was just up for a show? You will know if they are right for you when you don't feel support and encouragement about your own growth both emotionally and intellectually. The right person will want you to be emotionally healthy and able to stand on your own two feet. When you are with the right person you will feel good about yourself, safe, and fulfilled. The right person will not be negative, selfish, wishy-washy, silent, embarrassing, critical, or a slob. The right person is someone who you like and who is your friend. The right person will enjoy spending time with you. You and the right person will have similar goals and values in life. Having different likes and different opinions is okay if the two of you agree to disagree. Although you may not always agree with one another, conversations with the right person will be interesting and not boring. The right person will communicate thoughts and feelings with you and will not keep hurts and concerns bottled up inside. Understanding that the only constant in life is change, the right person is willing to discuss marriage, relationship issues, questions, and topics with you both before and after you get into a relationship or even get married. The right person is honest with you. The right person will trust you and not spy on you. And will not have you feeling as if you must justify your every move and become a very heavy burden. If you realize that there are red flags or problematic issues in your relationship, don't ignore them or delude yourself into thinking that the red flags aren't that important or that someone you love will change. It does take more than love to have a successful relationship.

But listen you don't have to listen to me to make decisions in your own life. We're not all meant for each other. And maybe that's ok. Sometimes they are there long enough to teach you the lessons that you need to learn. I'm just here to have you think about the unmistakable signs you may have overlook that will have you get into your own way of true happiness. Everyone always think they have a clear idea of the exact kind of person they want to fall in love with, but it is important to stay objective, to avoid getting attached too quickly. Remember my 30-60-90 Day Rule, I'm a big fan of dating multiple guys until you get exclusivity with one, so keep all options open. That's smart dating.

Follow your deepest inner intuition and knowing. This will help you make the right choices and dating & sleeping with the wrong person. People need to learn how to let go emotionally. Sometimes our emotions can be stubborn than thoughts. But let me say this our emotions can be the glue that holds us fast to our beliefs and expectations. Whenever we tell ourselves that we can't let go, were making an emotional statement. I found myself saying I can't all the time. Which really means I fear the emotional consequences if I do. My ego draws that line and insists that I will not survive my emotions that will arise if the line is crossed.

Remember chasing people around in life will be of no benefit to you in the long run. This is mostly because you can't make people be who you want them to be or with you. People will always do what they truly want to do, deep down inside. But what you can do is make extraordinary effort each day to be you, and to do whatever it is in your heart, working heard at it to make you happy. The people who deserve to be in your life will come in your life ultimately when it's right. But I think what we should have in mind is the signs of how to tell when a person is not ready for love. Really! There is always going to be red flags as plain as can be. But for some reason, we are not as observant when it comes to ourselves. We tell ourselves that we are ready to have a serious relationship regardless of the nagging voices in our heads. We blindly push forward ignoring our own warning signs and those of our friends and family. Unfortunately, ignoring the red flags is a sure-fire way to doom a relationship before it begins. Now when I say red flags. It's not the undesirable traits in the person you are dating. I'm talking about you. What is it about you that should warn others off you? In order to figure this out, you will need to take a hard look at yourself. There are always going to be warnings sign that you can recognize in yourself such as; pining, unhappy single, in a rush, and unstable.

Think about pining for a moment. If you are pining over an ex, you should not be dating. There is simply isn't room in a healthy relationship for a third person. Having someone new will not help you get over your ex. It will only confuse you and hurt the new person in your life. Keep in mind that relationships that start in this way are almost always doomed to failure.

If you are unhappy and single, you should take time to learn what it is that makes you happy. Never look to another person to make you happy. That's what is wrong with people nowadays. If you can't be content on your own, you will still be miserable in a relationship. Worse yet, you will make the person you are with miserable as well.

Ask yourself? Are you in a rush? Do you have an expiration date? If you are desperate to find a mate. Now, you have a problem and will end up choosing someone who is horrible for you. Finding the right person takes time. If you feel rushed, pull yourself out of the dating scene for a while. Just allow things to happen naturally.

Keep in mind If your life is unstable for many reasons, do not date. The reason could financial, spiritual or physical as in the case of illness. When you meet someone new, you want to be able to offer your best. If you are experiencing a vulnerable stage in your life, all while being single that has not been resolved, it is not fair to the other person to expect them to endure it with you. Because now your setting yourself up to be look at as damage goods. Having red flags or two does not means that you will never be able to date. It just means that you have things to work on. Just take some time to work on you. Learn all you can about yourself and what it takes to make you stable and happy. Once you have figured yourself out, you will be able to offer your best to the men or woman of your dreams.

At the end of the day, follow your deepest inner intuition and knowing. This will help guide you in making choices on dating and chasing people around in life will be no benefit to you in the long run. Because you can't make people be who you want them to be. People will always do what they want in the end. So be you, do you and work hard at it. The people who belong in your life will come in your life eventually.

MOVING FORWARD- END NOTES

My heart is my own. My spirit is my own. And I am in control of it. What I'm saying is, try to find a way to connect to yourself and live life beyond your wildest dreams. Love will follow.

MOVING FORWARD QUESTION.

What things make being in a relationship hard, and how do you push past them to get back to the love?

SECRETS & ANXIETY

If you thought that you were powerful to change reality think again.
Because our thoughts have the power to change our perception of reality and our perception has the power to manipulate it.

Can you see the simple signs that your energy is unbalanced?
What disturbance has caused your body, mind, spirit to be block and imbalance.
Because there are steps to healing after someone hurt you.
But I feel that there's so many things keeping you from finding love & living life.

Put yourself in someone else shoes.
Human beings are wired to run from pain.
What should I do? Take care of myself.
And that is in the best way for me.
My heart is my own. My spirit is my own.
I tell myself that with thoughts of depression & suicide.
Shit! We all thought it once or twice at one time.
Contemplating my next step. But Suicide is the not the way out.

Yeah! I'm pissed. I'm angry and sad.
Life is hard. Especially if your struggling and trying to survive & seeking love with so many problems & secrets.
The balance between good and evil has been tipped in favor of evil.

The truth I hold. Took me years to unfold.
Locked up and never told.
This pain I have will never go away or be healed, if I don't put myself first to fix it.

My world's crashing down on me.
No one should ever have to feel this way.
This pain I feel will be with me for a lifetime.

Pause! The Feelings of my heart race and pound fast, my anxiety kicks in.
Veins visible due to my anger and rage.
Tears rushing down my face, like its pouring down rain.
Standing here being drilled and question by people who know nothing of what I experience.
Be cautious with your approach.
Truth is; before you diagnose yourself with depression or low self-esteem. First make sure that you are not in fact just surrounded by assholes.
I just want to escape the torment and the negative thoughts haunting me.

I'm not crazy. But I know something is wrong.
I'm Just looking for release emotionally through my heavy burden on my heart, spirit, mind and soul.

So, pull up a chair and let's chat.
But leave your mix emotions at the door.
This ORA of unnatural balance to which I return.
Regardless of the decision made aid what happen in the past.
I found myself in an unlucky situation. Shit! Happens.
But let my story be a beacon of hope for someone whose now walk in my shoes.

Maybe I'm going about this all wrong.
These feelings I have of being stress & overwhelmed, guilty and totally unbalanced.
Anxiety really does have many overwhelming qualities.
Although I have a sense of duty to a greater civilization to change the world, one person, one community at a time.
I come first.

But I can't do that with negative energy surrounding me.
So, forgiveness right now is a process that takes time.
But in time, healing is a matter of breaking the dysfunctional patterns of thinking, feeling and behaving that are causing me distress.
I forgive you. I want you to be happy and move on.
This is your life and its been waiting for you to discover it.

Chapter Six

Rule #6. The Closure Rule. Forgive to release to move forward after breakups & move on from past relationships.

Reason, Season or Lifetime, this really puts things into perspective and makes you think about all sorts of past relationships and friendship. When you figure out which one it is, you will know what to do for each person. When someone is in your life for a reason, it is usually to meet a need you have expressed. They have come to assist you through a difficulty; to provide you guidance and support; to aid you physically, emotionally or spiritually. They may seem like a godsend, and they are. They are there for the reason you need them to be. Some people come into your life for a season, because your turn has come to share, grow or learn. They bring you an experience of pace or make you laugh. They may teach you something you have never done. They usually give you an unbelievable amount of joy. Believe it. It is real. But only for a season. Lifetime relationships teach your lifetime lessons; things you must build upon to have a solid emotional foundation. Your job is to accept the lesson, love the person and put what you have learned to use in all other relationships and areas of your life. It is said that love is blind in other relationships and areas of your life, it is also said that love is blind, but friendship is clairvoyant. But I wrote this closure rule to tell people. Move own and get past the past jealousy. All it is, is anxiety about your past relationship that threatens your current relationship, which you keep dwelling on it. Don't think you're crazy because you have these feelings. But don't turn your relationship or the person you're trying to get to know into a trial either. Try to minimize interrogation, reassurance seeking, accusation, and withdrawing. These strategies only make matters worse. Relationships end because they were either unrewarding or you were no longer important to that person. Move forward and try not to resurrect the past to get on with your life. Just focus on making the present better.

When someone you care about hurts you, you can't hold on to anger, resentment and thoughts of revenge or embrace forgiveness and move forward. Who hasn't been hurt by the actions or words of another? But if you don't practice forgiveness, you might be the one who pays most dearly. By embracing forgiveness, you can also embrace peace, hope, gratitude and joy. Consider how forgiveness can lead you down the path of physical, emotional and spiritual well-being.

Forgiveness can even lead to feelings of understanding, empathy and compassion for the one who hurt you. Forgiveness doesn't mean forgetting or excusing the harm done to you or making up with the person who caused the harm. Forgiveness brings a kind of peace that helps you go on with life. Why do people always bring up the history? When people hear complaints when in a relationship or trying to date someone for the first time, they get look at as negative, bringing up the past as never stopping, never letting things go when you try to attempt to make things better or just trying to get to know someone without being judge from their past. The biggest reason anyone holds on to the past is because they don't feel heard or fully understood by the person, they perceived hurt them. You can do this by naming your emotions, and not putting yourself into a situation by just listening to the person experience. Our grudge morphs into a boulder that blocks the light of kindness from reaching our heart, and thus is an obstacle to true healing. Sadly, in its effort to garner us empathy, our grudge ends up depriving us of the very empathy that we need to release it.

The idea is not to re-traumatize us by diving into the original pain but rather to attend to it with the compassion that we didn't receive, that our grudge is screaming for, and bring it directly into the center of the storm. Our heart contains both our pain and the elixir for our pain. To let go of a grudge we need to move the focus off the one who "wronged" us, off the story of our suffering, and into the felt experience of what we lived. When we move our attention inside, into our heart, our pain shifts from being a "something" that happened to us, another part of our narrative, to a sensation that we know intimately, a felt sense that we are one with from the inside.

What we need to know about the rule of forgiveness is that it's a voluntary process. We can win if we truly let go. Life is too short. Sometime we hold on too long to what a person did to us that we fail to see the signs and symptoms of what it's really doing to our mind, body and soul. Who wants to feel empty and lifeless? Depression is a serious killer. Or shall I say a chemical imbalance that slowly cause us to lose it and commit suicide or even turn to drugs, alcohol or sex. My words may come off a little bit harsh, but I encourage victims to unleash the power within to remove personal roadblocks. I know that forgiveness is a process and it takes time. The first step is often just knowing that you want to be able to forgive someone at some point. When we forgive, we're not saying that we were never hurt, that it didn't matter and that we're going to forget all about the hurt. We're more saying that we're no longer going to hold whatever happened against the other person. Although it seems like when we do that, we're giving them a gift or letting them win, but we reap the benefits even more! By using the rule of forgiveness, we break all rules by moving on and letting go negative emotions, fully and truly loving again, laughing and smiling uncontrollably. It's a struggle to control your emotions, but once you find a way you will be able to maintain and move on. Trust is easy to take for granted. It's your duty to tell the truth even when you know the truth may hurt and possibly even cost you your friendship. I can honestly say I don't have true friends. To me a true friend is someone you can rely on. There have been plenty of self-less moments where I have sacrificed my own comfort and happiness and put others first. And when I needed supportive friends or even family members, they was nowhere around when you needed them the most. No one knows what might happen in the future or the next minute in your life, yet still we try to move forward, because we have faith.

We all make mistakes at time and break the golden rule of being true friends. Forgiveness doesn't mean you're minimizing your victimization experience. It just bring more awareness to the fact that you may have friends that are so involved into their own lives that they may have overlook the fact that you've been neglected, victimized and no one understands the trauma you face was very bad and real. We must not be afraid to be honest with people. Forgiveness is not a moment in time that simply makes things better. But a process that takes time and important, extreme self-awareness. When we embrace the journey of forgives, only then do we begin to heal. It's also good to have a good friend in our lives that plays a significant role as a social supporter to reduce health problems including, depression etc. What it does is boost our happiness and reduce stress so we can have a sense of belonging and purpose.

We need to understand guilt causes anger and resentment not only at yourself, but toward others to justify your actions. Anger, resentment and guilt sap your energy, cause depression and illness and prevent success, pleasure and fulfilling relationships. They keep you stuck in the past and prevent you from moving forward. You may feel guilty not only for your actions, but also your thoughts, lack of feelings, such as reciprocal love or friendship. I'm not calling anyone friends fake. I'm just simply stating in your time of need and support; you can distinguish the difference between a real friend and fake friends. But the rule of forgiveness is to release ourselves from the hold a person has on us and move forward. Deep inside still exist the little beacon of hope that shows we have the strength and courage to live and fight and to take back hold of our lives. People need to understand the psychological damage it creates. And that there's an after effect that leaves in the victim's love life? Leaving us to be hyper-vigilance and distance from people. To the victim, you can't point fingers at everyone and anyone which affects you and others that don't support you in all your endeavors. Just trust the power of forgiveness to heal the hurt and pain, instead allowing it to eat at you.

MOVING FORWARD- END NOTES

Forever feeling tired, and helpless. No one should ever have to experience something like this. But this is a secret a lot of people are holding in. Afraid to talk about. We need to forgive to release to let go in order to move forward. This is the first step in reconnecting to yourself.

MOVING FORWARD QUESTIONS.

There's nothing wrong with venting, pouring out one's troubles to an empathic ear. But I encourage anyone to seek professional counseling about dealing with specific set of issues. They will help you work through difficult issues. So, think about spreading your business to family & friends. Because messy people will talk about you behind your back and spread your business to only make your situation worse. #IMNOTCRAZY

MOVING FORWARD- END NOTES

All the world's a stage. And all the men and women merely actors, playing many parts. So, you decide to audition for a role in my life, i.e.; Approach & Date me. Thing is; What roles & rules are you playing with me today? Because I did not cast, nor audition you bitch.

TROPHY

Is that what I am to you? You're Trophy.
Displaced there clearly on your mantle, so all can see.

Yeah, I see your jaw dropped. You got me fuck up.
Feeling like damaged goods for having sex to early.
My exposed mistake that has permanently changed my reputation and my life.

Psychological manipulation. You tried to control me by my fears, lies, obligation and guilt.
Are you gaslighting me? Trying to twist my memories and thoughts.
Making up things that never happened.
To have me feel like I know longer know what is real.

Who lies & makes themselves emotionally unavailable due to unfortunate circumstances in the past?
Paying the price for your mistakes.
And show case my downfalls and magnify my mistakes.
How guilty are you?

This applied tool of manipulation is just a distraction, from me trying to heal and move on.
Nope! I'm moving forward & trying to heal. My future significant other will not experience my baggage and pay for my mistakes of being emotionally damage from the past by you.
Damage goods tend to run away from their problems instead of facing them head on.

Tell them, that you cheated me out my most valuable prize.
Fooled me and filled me up with all your lies.
Tricked by you, to let you in, to fool me out my precious gift.
Was I ready? Were you the one? I don't know.

Many people confuse love, commitment and sex or assume the three always go hand in hand.
But sexual relationships work best when everybody is clear about what they want. But I was young.

This twister of feelings, raging inside me.
Countless showers can't even wash away what I feel.
This ORA of guilt, sadness I feel inside for you.
Come close. Let me show you what it feels like.
To have your luck taken by the devilish leprechaun.
My trophy, this piece of gold.
Trick by you, to let you in and be taken.

Look deep into my eyes to see that I'm stain for life.
Used for sex and then kick to the curb.
This feeling of guilt, sadness in my heart.
A stain I can't wash off. Sex is complicated and personal.
No one can tell you when you're ready, but we are pressure into it.
Just try to remember, you oversee your own life.
The education goes out the door when love has you blind.
Hundreds of millions of people are infected with sexually transmitted diseases if not careful.

I can't find peace of mind because of you.
There is no rewinds, no turning back.
All I can do is think. Is that what I am to you?
You're used trophy. Displayed there on a fucking mantle so all can see.
This piece of gold, my most valuable prize.

My mind, body and soul is fuel by anger.
But I'd not let it consume me. Let rage not fuel itself into blows to become only regret and shame.
Let me not run to rage with eager toes.

Burning anger that silences everything around me and yet I can feel nothing.
Damn, this guy played some serious head games on me.
But waiting to have sex is not easy these days. Even when you go by the 30-60-90-day rules.

Changes can have a huge impact on your life and trigger distress or make it worse.
My heart dies a slow death, shedding each hope like leaves until one day there are none. No hope, nothing remains.

I'm nobody trophy boy.
I'm a keeper. Someone's treasure.

Chapter Seven

Rule #7. Relationships are tricky. Whatever you are willing to accept is exactly what you're going to get. It all about the 80/20 rule.

Sometimes, our lives can change so fast that the change outpaces our mind and hearts. It's those times, I think, when our lives have been altered, & bad things happen, we long for the time before everything was altered or change. But relationships are a tricky bugger. Whatever you are willing to accept is exactly what you're going to get. But what makes us happy or unhappy? I finally realized that beyond the discontentment that often drives us to despair or to think we are unhappy is a deeper wisdom that that tells us that, "You may just be unhappy. Or in the wrong place with the wrong person, or in the wrong place experiencing a situation in an environment at a present time were trying to change. But remember your unhappiness may be a temporary phase, an overload of the current pressures of life or a need to recognize self-neglect. It may be that you need to take a step back and evaluate yourself and how you have "de-animated" much of your life. Perhaps, over time, you gradually withdrew your enthusiasm, and you never even realized it. We often de-animate relationships, jobs, everything and anything, and because it happens so gradually, that we don't discover who we are deeply until we are so low on energy that our entire life looks bleak, bringing you disharmony to your house or your personal spirit. That the most effective solution is to simply end a relationship.

When it comes to relationships, the people you hang out with affect your happiness the most: i.e.; friends or dating partner etc. Listen, "Do 20% of your friends or partners provide 80% of support and enjoyment?" Knowing which friend or partner your dating bring you joy, allows you to enjoy spending time with them and truly understand that they care about you, so you can shift the time spent on certain relationships that truly matters. Have you once practiced the 80/20 in your life and applied the 80/20 principle over the years to affirmed certain values that you set for yourself? Like Relationships, Habits, and Daily Life. Let's take a look at these three issues for a moment.

Relationships. *Over the years, I realized that while I have many people on my social networks, 80% of my enjoyment comes from a few key individuals. Thus, I focus more on developing these relationships, while reducing time from the relationships that drain me.*

Habits. *I cultivate the few key habits that make the most difference in my life: (a) waking up early, (b) meditating, and (c) healthy eating. Though these habits look very simple to you. They bring along a huge host of benefits. After cultivating them, I'm much more productive, focused, and happier. I also know that by practicing them, I'm improving my health and potential life span.*

Daily Life. *After reflecting on my daily activities, I found that I'm most inspired when I'm in nature and when I'm connected with like-minded individuals. I seek out meetups and opportunities to connect with people who share the same interests. At the same time, I'm constantly removing tasks that drain me. Doing this, I get more value out of my everyday life. Life becomes much more fulfilling and rewarding.*

This is where I turn the 80/20 rule for relationships on its head and add my own twist. The 80 percent of the issues we have with others are our own internal battles. 20 percent are actual relationship issues. To get to that crucial twenty percent, you must first work through your own baggage. Otherwise, you spend all your time bogged down in your own internal issues, never getting to the 20 percent that is vital to creating a meaningful relationship. I believe the reason why so many of us don't feel fulfilled and good enough in the relationship is because we are in denial or unaware of our own internal battles that's been surfacing and showing up on the scene. It has absolutely nothing to do with our partner. It's you. The 80/20 Rule states that in most healthy long-term relationships, you only get about 80 per cent of what you need/want from your current partner. This is because no one is perfect. When you have two different individuals with diverse backgrounds and personality. There bond to be problems. But if you're well matched, you're both respectful of one another, loving, and share a lot of the same interests. This is the 80%. Bottom-line, there is that one thing your partner lacks, which in turn your new partner is supposed to come in and fulfilled - this is the 20%. Some say for men, the missing 20% is usually sex, time and attention or money for women. But really, it could be anything.

I also say just use the rule to improve what relationship you're in. And, in order to make your relationship better by making use of this 80 20 rule, you should address 20% of the problems that cause 80% of the frustrations in your relationship. That way, you can sort those more noticeable problems in your relationship. And if you have problems follow my 5 Step Process for relationship during dating phase in order to reach the higher phases, especially if significant problems arise such as; insecurity, mistrust, infidelity, immaturity, emotional withdrawal, anger issues, and or abuse. Dating is a process that, if not done properly, can lead to a loving, lasting relationship. All problems can be worked through with patience, and love. Just remember my phases 1-6 and you will be alright.

Phase 1 – Getting to know you. *During this phase, each person is free to date multiple people, without commitment. Significant physical contact will be limited.*
Phase 2 –Friends with benefits. *During this phase, a couple may have identified one person with whom they decided to engage in significant physical contact. They are still free to go out with other people; however, significant physical contact is limited to that one person.*

Phase 3 – Monogamous Dating. *During this phase, two people have decided that they want to pursue a relationship and end all other dating. During this phase, the foundation of the relationship is established, introductions to family takes place, and the beginnings of commitment and accountability are established.*

Phase 4 – Pre-Marital. *During this phase, the couple will engage in exercises that deepen their level of intimacy. Communication is key. Expectations are established, goals and dreams are discussed, and the future of the relationship becomes visible. Remember, at this phase, what you see is what you get. If things aren't right at this phase, they won't get better on their own.*

Phase 5 – Long-Term Consistency Dating. *Sparking chemistry with a new partner is a powerful, but it's a temporary feeling sometimes. Couples will inevitably face hardship and must make tough decisions and will run into conflict. And what's going to get a couple through that? Consistency. We know that chemistry is necessary and good because it creates the desire and is part of the relationship game. However, consistency must take over for that relationship to succeed. You want to trust that they will always be there for you. You know that through the good and bad times they will be standing beside you. You shouldn't have to sit there wondering or analyzing things because you don't know or aren't sure of their feelings or intentions. You will know. Relationships should run smoothly. No doubt you will have some bumps in the road, but they should be things that you can work through. When someone is consistent then you know what to expect, it provides stability and you know* *where you stand. It's simple really. Why would you want anything less?*

Phase 6 – Marriage. *The commitment is made, roles and responsibilities are established, and the work of the relationship begins.*

I wish I knew back then what I now know, but you live and learn right! I believe that there should be one and only one partner for life. Engaging in sexual activity with someone other than your 'partner' is morally wrong and 'unnatural'. I refuse to accept anything less than the 80/20 rule. Unlike my best friend who believe in the 888 rule. He's says there 8 hours of work, 8 hours of rest and 8 hours of devotion to the other half. Thinking about the expanse of time through all the physical distance from your partners you encounter. It forces you to learn clear and open communication. Those experiences has brought you close as humans, partners and lovers. Ask yourself this? What have you've learned? I've learned to never waste an opportunity to correct a problem in the relationship, to always share what's on their minds and to be vulnerable in front each other. They have learned the power of honesty, forgiveness an unconditional love.

No one should have to feel, that they don't deserve anything less or question their relationship to see if it measures up. When I was with Ricco, one of my past love. I had felt deep down inside the relationship was not going to work out. He was not giving me the full 80 per cent of what I needed and want from him. I tried to address the 20 per cent of the issues that cause 80 per cent of the frustration in the relationship. But for some reason I stayed and dealt with the bull shit. I was in an unhealthy relationship thinking I could turn it into a healthy relationship. I don't know what the fuck I was thinking. Whatever you are willing to accept is exactly what you're going to get. One of the most prevalent themes of pain and loss throughout the course of human history is being cheated on. There are few greater pains than believing that you are in a loving, monogamous relationship and then finding out through some source that this is not the case. Being cheated on can undermine the trust and even the love in a relationship. Especially if cheating was not expected, it can cause extremely strong emotions such as hurt and betrayal. Deep down inside it is that voice of truth that's always giving us what we need to hear and see? But do we really listen.

I do know relationships are a tricky bugger. I can't change what happened with me and all the men I met, and even if I could, I wouldn't want to. Life is all about learning experiences. But what I have learn is to not let my past relationship traumas hold me back. I have learned to let go of the fear, accept the possibility that the next person I meet could be a good guy. Keep in mind when applying the 80/20 rule in a relationship, there were probably common mistakes I probably made as well with Ricco. It does takes two partners to create a relationship. So, it was unfair for me to dish out every negative aspect on him. Maybe my standards should have been lower a little bit more to change my current views in orders to achieve a compromise with him. But that doesn't change the fact that Ricco cheated on me. This 80/20 rule should be used wisely. Maybe me withholding sex to get to know him more was my way of controlling the relationship. And when things got hard for him in the relationship or his sex addiction or urges got stronger. The 20 per cent stood out more and what little he had to offer was appealing and attractive to someone else. Nevertheless, that should not be an excuse to cheat and jump from one wagon to another, because that next person may not have that 80 to 100 per cent of what your need. No! I won't accept that. If you was unhappy, that should have been communicated and I would have ended the relationship.

MOVING FORWARD- END NOTES

The most fucked up thing in the world. Is someone who says he'll love you forever and ever? Say you're his world. And you turn around and find him fucking somebody else behind your back.

MOVING FORWARD QUESTIONS.

What makes a relationship last? Is it sex? Or is it (communication, trust, loyalty, etc.)?

WAKE UP CALL

Listen.
Can't you see what's wrong?
Sadness, anger, pain, it hurts.

We wear the mask.
Our problems, fears and secrets.
Are stored, locked and hidden.
From the people around us.

Judging us with their dark and unknowing eyes.
Were haunted by the thoughts of what people are thinking.

Blinded by the reality of me.
I'm just trying to be me.
One's self-image is destroy (Why!)

Because we felt like we were losing their approval.
We felt invisible.
Now look at us.
Approach with "Extreme caution".
People think were crazy now.
Because we felt victim, becoming their easy target.

Dam this feeling as if you're standing on the edge of a cliff.
You can't help but to feel off balance because of it.
I am afraid.
Afraid of letting go.
Afraid of my life.
Afraid to show emotions.
Afraid that I might seek revenge.
I'm afraid you're wrong.
This is a fear of falling.
Love and let be loved.
This is your finally wake up call.

Chapter Eight

Rule# 8. The Basic Rule of Love. Follow the personal code of Trust, Respect, Communication for a happier life.

The Rules of Love: A Personal Code for Happier, More Fulfilling Relationships with your best friend or partner is Trust, Respect, & Communication. Everyone needs a superhero to trust & challenge them now and again. Because the truth is, we are all scared of falling in love and getting hurt. We are all scared of losing someone we love. We are all scared of breaking someone's heart while trying to mend ours own. But if we keep looking for all the reasons why love can be scary, we will keep our hearts in a cage forever. And our hearts are made to be broken sometimes. They're made to fly, and to be set free. So, stop putting your walls up, pushing people away, and building barriers to prevent you from falling in love. You can keep saying you're scared, not ready or not sure, but then one day your going to meet someone and somehow they will make you ready, they make you less scared of falling in love, they will make you want to open up and live. They will make you understand how sometimes there's just no logic in love, but it will make perfect sense in the end. So, no one is totally ready and you're probably not either, but that wasn't, isn't and will never be a reason to stop you or anyone else from falling in love. Remember everyone goes through trials in their life. But its your job to know the truth. The truth of who you are. So, let the truth set you free, because every decision you ever made, led you to the right space and place in your life. And you got there because you relied on that inner voice.

Remember, a fulfilling relationship is when both individuals contribute to each other's happiness, but without any expectations. You are the one who decides for yourself if you are happy or unhappy. Don't put that decision on your partner. Remember, your partner can only contribute to your happiness. You want a safe, equal, and emotionally intimate relationship, which's means that you aren't constantly taking care of the other person. If you are always looking at how to please the other person, responding to their difficulties daily, and/or helping them manage their emotions, then your relationship is probably more of a caretaker. Being a caretaker can feel safe because you are in control and don't have to risk vulnerability of equal give and take. If you don't expect to have someone who shares in the problem-solving, then you aren't disappointed. You may love the person and cherish the connection. You may want the person in your life forever and there is great value in that it just isn't an emotionally equal relationship. In an equal relationship neither person is the caretaker and both care for and nurture the relationship and each other.

Love someone not because of what you can get, but what you can give. You may fall in love due to selfish reasons and fall out of love when there are no personal gains. Do not just fall in love because you can easily fall out of love when the things you desire no longer exist in your relationship. Ensure you love someone completely – for who he/she is, embrace each other's flaws, see and bring the best out of each other, during good and bad seasons of your journey and be patient with each other. Let your love for each other grow beyond measures. That's the secret to unlocking the key to love here.

*Here's the key: The Rules of Love: A Personal Code for a Happier, More Fulfilling Relationships is with **TRUST, RESPECT & COMMUNICATION.** Trust is something that grows. If you take some time to think about trust, what it really means is that to feel safe to share your thoughts, emotions and body with another person, without fearing that he will betray you; that doesn't mean cheating necessarily, but rather he won't intentionally do anything that makes you feel unvalued or like you can't open up fully and take down your guard.*

Imagine trust as a garden that needs tending. Early on in dating, you're given a packet of seeds, a rusty tin can of water, and some dirt. You need to invest time, energy, and faith. You need to keep watering your garden and tend to it, remaining faithful that the seeds will bloom. The benefits you will reap from all the energy and love you put into your garden will come in time, but though they might not be apparent at first, it doesn't mean that they are not on their way. When you've been dating someone for a few weeks, or even a few months, you will need to be patient, as your partner might take longer than you to figure out his feelings and what he really wants. This is not to say that you wait for an eternity for someone to declare that he only wants to be with you, but rather, that there is a transitional period between being single and meeting someone great. Often, it takes some time to adjust to opening and being in a relationship. It can take time to work out communicating with a new partner and figuring out a new partner's triggers, boundaries, likes and dislikes. Imagine if you were dating a man whose previous girlfriend didn't like to talk or share her feelings. It might take some getting used to for him to adjust to someone who does like to communicate and share things. Similarly, behaviors that might not have bothered a past partner might bother you, and so there is a period of learning that requires grace and faith. The trick is to keep planting seeds of trust, encourage your partner to be open and communicative, and be patient while he sorts through his feelings and desires. Encourage him to share his truth, even if he thinks it will hurt your feelings, and be willing to be honest even when it's uncomfortable.

Second, Respect is a personal code for a happier relationship. Casual dating still involves having a relationship with someone, and respect is important in any relationship: casual, serious, or somewhere in between. That means treating the person with the same kindness you'd treat any other human being just without the commitment. If you're no longer into someone, even casually, you can do one of two things: Stop asking them to do stuff and hope they go away (and they might) or tell them you're just not feeling it anymore when they say they want to hang out. If he doesn't seem interested in you, don't chase him. No matter how you try to kid yourself, you know all too well when a guy just isn't interested. He might not explicitly tell you to get lost, but his actions will. If a man's ignoring your calls, being purposely distant, or putting in the minimum effort, you can be all but certain that he's not after you. Stop chasing him. Begging him to be your guy is just plain embarrassing and you're better than that. Respect yourself and move on.

Respect is important in all human relationships. If you can't respect someone for what they've done, you can give them basic human respect. Respect is especially important in love relationships. Because lasting love relationships help define who you are as a person, it's crucial that the relationship is a healthy one. When you and your partner respect each other, you create a healthy relationship in which you can both mature and gain personal strength throughout your lifetimes. When you fail to respect your partner, you bar the way from getting honest respect from them in return. Your failure creates an environment in which your partner can't be their best. Just as important, you put yourself in that same environment, where love is more like a disease and a burden to both of you. When you truly love someone, you want the best for them. If you want to give them your best, it stands to reason that you have to give them your utmost respect. How do you do that? You do it by the way you think about them, express yourself, and behave towards them.

Third, Communicating & being honest in a relationship means you tell the truth. If you are lying, that puts a barrier between you and the other person. Maybe ask yourself the reason you are lying. Are you hiding who you truly are? Are you hiding because of your own judgments or is it likely that the other person will reject or criticize you if they know the truth? If you are lying, then the relationship loses intimacy and safety. Being honest doesn't mean the same as passing judgement or making assumptions or giving an unsolicited opinion. Being honest is not saying something hurtful because you are hurt. Being honest means, you express your emotions accurately and in a loving way. You stay on the same side. You don't blame, name-call, or use the relationship to control what the other person does. Emotional honesty, factual honesty and respect support and nurture loving connections. People often confuse communication for talking or making conversation, and this is the root cause of why many of these same people are so unsuccessful in communicating with their partners. Communication in relationships, at its core, is about connecting and using your verbal, written and physical skills to fulfill your partner's needs – not just making small talk.

How many times have you truly been in love? I know it's been to many times for me. After the pain and suffering of being heart broken. The problem is trying to find love in our dating lives. There are common mistakes we make such as not finding characteristics in a person. Instead we look at physical appearance, popularity, or wealth. These are not the qualities that God looks at and neither should we. But when you have a good person, stand firm and strong and ride that ruff storm, because it could be meant to be if you seek counseling to resolve your issue.

We need to stand firm through the wind of life and believe that all things are possible. It we can only believe that love is a natural wonderful feeling and that it is so powerful that it can also cause us pain. There will never be any proper advice on how to deal with the kind of pain it inflicts. Love hurts when there is no right foundation, when trust is betrayed, when there is no respect and when love is lost. It hurts us because we are human beings and nothing can ever prepare us for it, because it just comes out naturally even without inviting it into our lives.

Love creates an overwhelming feeling that envelopes us and makes us very protective of the love we have. It hurts because we don't stop thinking of ways to keep the love burning, to keep it safe. It is even more devastating when efforts prove to become futile when the love you give is not reciprocated. You can never win in the game of love, when there is only one side of it. It is truly the saddest part of love. Love knows no boundaries and I wish we all should be aware of this. We simply cannot avoid getting hurt, but as they say, 'it is better to love than to have never loved at all'. David use to say those words to me all the time. Encouragement when he felt as if I was losing hope. And every time I heard those words. I just knew it was better for me to fight for something than live for nothing. There's always something or someone in your life worth fighting for. Stand up people and fight for love and our equal rights. We have come a long way in recent years, but there's still a long way to go. No matter what we do or say. There will always be a long-life struggle and argument on gay rights.

Remember when you do find someone cherish every moment in life with them. Life is unpredictable. Cherish the moments even when you fall out of love. Remember those good moments that brought you two together, hoping to only re-spark the flame that burns inside you both, rekindling your love all over if it's meant to be. I encourage you to stand firm through the winds of life and know that you can make it together as a whole if you stand firm together.

MOVING FORWARD--END NOTES

It's true that our obstacles and suffering shapes us for greatness. If we run from it, you will never learn to face it. We can't control faith. But always remember its part of life.

FAKE BITCH! FAKE FRIEND!

Fake Bitch! Fake Friend. Same thing.

Where are the real genuine honest people at?
The ones who's always honest, genuine, uplifting and looking for a lesson in every negative situation or failures.
Finding new ways to do better.

I'm a very intuitive person.
I try to avoid the traps of fakeness and to be tuned to the understanding of my choices that are good and not so good.

Fake Bitch! Fake Friend. Same thing.
Be careful who you share your weaknesses & dreams too.
Some people can't wait for the opportunity to use them against you.

I have a tolerance limit and when you reach it, I will dismiss you from my life.
It's that simple.

People like to see you do well, but not better than them.
Some people will pretend to care just so they can get a better seat to watch your struggles.
Every helping hand isn't always there to help.
Sometimes you just need to distance yourself from people.

If they care they'll notice.
If they don't, you know where you stand.
True friends aren't the ones who make your problems disappear.
But fake friends are the ones who will appear when your facing problems.

We all want that feeling of certainty that everything is ok and that all your basic needs will be provided for.

Security means the state of being free from danger or threat. Danger means the possibility of suffering harm or injury. The possibility of something unwelcome or unpleasant happening to us is alarming. Have you at least questioned someone's personal motives? Whether they be faulty malicious or intentional misjudgment?

Meeting new people and making friends can be overwhelming, but with a little effort and willingness to step outside of your comfort zone, you can easily make friends. But be careful, fake bitch, fake friend. You cant tell these days anymore.

Hmm! I don't know. Is it that easy!
Why am I stuck in a generation where loyalty is just a tattoo?
Love is just a quote & Lying is the new truth.

Wherever you go, be it in the real world, because you will come across two types of people "fake" and "genuine." But remember toxic friendships are negative relationships that make you feel unhappy, unhealthy, and unequal. A little gossip or venting can be a healthy thing in moderation. But when it enters a kind of relentless and mean-spirited state, trying to tear a person down. Then we have a serious problem.
Bitch! You in danger gurl.
We may need to throw them hands.
Its either me or you bitch. And I choose me first.

They say we must be forgiving & selfless in a selfish world.

How many times have you seen someone be used for financial disparity when there down on their luck?
Financial disparity! There I said it.

So, you have money and know your purpose. But what give you the right to become bored & dismiss people who aren't doing the same thing yet.

Yes! It could become awkward if you and your friends can't afford the same travel arrangements, restaurants and other entertainments.
It may be difficult, but don't let these negative imposters bring you down.

Those are the same fake friends, standing behind you in clubs waiting for you to pay their cover fee into clubs, pick up the drink tab, but have their own money.
So, we buying friendship now?
The same traveling friends waiting for you to pick up the restaurant tab or hotel room fees.
Who think a cute face, thin waist, six pack abs should be an integral component of the gay culture? Shit! Any culture that gets them advantages in life.
Even the fittest guys have body issues
They will never be happy if they continue to search for what happiness consists of.
You can never be happy at the expense of the happiness of others,

Let's downshift & work towards simple living by making conscious choices to leave materialism behind and move on to a more sustainable lifestyle.
It does not mean simply cutting back and trying to live the same life only with less money.
Frugal living isn't about living as cheaply as you can.

Rather, it's about making mindful choices that allows you to save money so that you can pay off your debt faster and enjoy the small and big things in life when it's your time.

Now I'm not blaming all for my shitty as life!
Preparation meets opportunity which equals success.
Its not an overnight success for some.
Not all happiness is created equal.
But be careful who you share your weaknesses, dreams and hard moments too.
It will either scar every fake person in your life away or it will inspire them to finally let go of that mirage called "perfection".
Which will open the doors to the most important relationships your ever be a part of.

Remember, there will be times when you face obstacles with fake bitches in your life.
But find a way to look past all the hardship and continue to dig deep to find courage to be able to face something alone.
Because despite life detours, you are destined for greatness.
So, when that fake person or so call friend say, your jealous, calls you worthless or a nobody, angry or nasty. Picks on you because you don't have the fancy car or clothes or luxury apartment. Nope! Your mistaken.
This is me being resolute for my security and standing firmly in my truth.
Trying to avoid the traps of fakeness.
Trying to remember that some people aren't loyal to you.
They are loyal to their need of you.
And once their needs change, so does their loyalty.

Chapter Nine

Rule#9. The Rule of Friendship is to be Real, Support & Encourage, but Live in Your Truth & do not allow your fears to Rule your Life from meeting a new Love or Friend.

No matter how old we get, fake friends can put deep scars on our hearts and big dents in our confidence. I have known this truth for as long as I have tried to make a friend or two, but each time I face it, I feel a sting. Give carefully when you give your friendship to others. If someone blows you off or lets you down, quickly remind yourself that person was not a real friend in the honest sense of friendship. Therefore, they are neither worth your time nor your energy.

Stop trying to change yourself to please other people. Friendship have a huge impact on your mental health and happiness. Good friends relieve stress, provide comfort, joy and prevent loneliness and isolation. Many of us struggle to meet people and develop quality connection. What we don't want to do is turn acquaintances into friends. Self-disclose: The small talk or trade jokes or insight with your personal stuff. Friendship is characterized by intimacy. True friends know about each other values. Struggles, goals and interests. You don't have to reveal your most closely held secrets to acquaintances. But do not let that stop you from overcoming obstacles to make new friends. Developing and maintaining friendship take time and effort. So just because someone isn't interested in talking or hanging out doesn't automatically mean there rejecting you as a person. Making a new friend is just the beginning of the journey. Have realistic expectations when it comes to what you expect from people you would call friend. Change your expectations to keep yourself from wanting too much and from giving too much. Everyone has lives they have to attend to, and no one can be everything for everyone. Be honest with yourself. If you feel you have more bad times than good times with another person, reassess the pros and cons of keeping the friendship alive. It may be time to end the relationship or it may be time to retune it until it becomes something better. Work on being resilient, telling yourself you will survive and in fact thrive, no matter if someone drops your friendship or decides they don't want to be your friend in the first place. In other words, don't let someone else's decision about a mutual friendship define whom you are or what you have to offer. Anyone who has had close friendship knows that while these relationships are rewarding, they often require hard work to maintain.

Especially when you try to find a way through the chaos of these head strong personalities of these crazy zodiacs signs.

How well do you know your friends, and how well can you tell real and fake friends apart in your life? Truth be told, your ultimate security and joy lies in knowing which friends are "friends indeed" and which ones are "fair-weather friends." If you have been struggling to differentiate real and fake friends in your life, this piece will serve as the ultimate guide you need to tell friends apart from today's fake ones. A real fiend is like family. A blood brother/sister. A real friend always inspires the confidence of a blood brother in you. He feels like family. You see him as "a brother from another mother." You don't get this feeling with a fake friend; you see him as an outsider or an acquaintance at best. A real friend acts, thinks, and carries on as an original member of your family tree and relatives nearly see him as such, but a fake friend will remain an ordinary friend of yours to family members. Just think when obstacles inevitably arise, we sometimes need a little help keeping our goals in perspective. The people in your support network will be there for you when you need to talk after a long day, or when you're feeling overwhelmed with work, school or your other obligations. Supportive friends, family, professors and colleagues will celebrate your successes and help you learn from your failures, providing the encouragement that you need to meet each challenge with determination and a positive attitude.

Live in your Truth and do not allow it to Rule your life from meeting a new love or friends. Right now, people are out here fighting a fight against homophobia, stigma, unfair beliefs and discrimination against gay, bisexual and other men who have sex with men which affects the health and well-being of the gay people in our community. It's bad enough people have attitude toward gay people. And that attitude can lead to rejection by friends and family, discriminatory acts and violence and laws and policies with negative consequences. Many of our young people are committing suicide, bullied and forced from their homes due to family rejection of their actual or perceived sexual orientation or gender identity. If we can't have a good social support from family, friends, and the gay community, to have a high self-esteem, a more positive group identity and more positive mental health. Then who can we turn to. Because gay people already have a bunch of gay cliques or mean boys like jocks, otter, bears or wolf etc. who use descriptive terms to be identified and labeled. Life is hard to live let alone having the fear to fit in or even come out as a gay man. Because our fears, no matter what they are, dictate how we live our lives each day, even if we don't realize it. Letting people down is a strange fear. Even though I have yet met someone who's able to live in their truth and admit their fear and what they are afraid of. But I can see myself with that fear. My fear simply means that I care what others think of me. It means that I will put someone else's needs and wants in front of my own. It means that I find it hard to say no to helping someone when I'm struggling to help myself. What if I'm not good enough? What if I fail? How would they look at me differently? These are a few of the constant questions that run through my mind. It affects how I interact with others or how I act. If I'm really my full self, will anyone still like me? My fear may seem irrational to you, while your greatest fear could mean nothing to me. If I'm afraid of rejection, afraid of letting someone down, and afraid of not being good enough. That means I don't branch out often. I put others before myself, which isn't always a bad thing, but you need to help yourself every now and then. I try to be who others wanted me to be, versus being myself. Maybe it was me having bad confidence, maybe it's just that I like to make others happy, or simply know what it feels like to be let down. Regardless of my fear, I know what I'm afraid of. I know that

I have probably let others down and I will continue to let others down. But I know I will never be perfect because people are naturally imperfect. Our fears can define who we are and how we live our lives, it's not until we realize what those fears are, that it teaches us to face them, to step forward courageously with confidence to overcome what terrifies us the most. But I will not let my fears affect my life anymore. I can't please everyone, but I can be happy with who I am.

Live in your truth. Your truth serves as your roadmap, it is your guiding force, your light and beacon to navigate your way ahead. While we make daily choices that guide our life's path, living in accordance with our truth is the highest choice we make. What you accept as your truth becomes your destiny. Your truth influences your beliefs, thus impelling your actions. I truly believe at a deeper level we are striving to do the best we can, given the resources available to us at the time. Your level of awareness shapes your life. The veils falls away when we can express the growing awareness of the truth. And the truth is revealed when we learn not to hold on to grudges or anger. There may be times when we unwittingly offend others through our choices and actions. If we abide by our truth, we trust that we cannot please everyone and therefore if we act morally and dutifully, we are following our deepest wisdom. I am not suggesting our truth harm or offend others. As we live our truth, it should unite others toward a common goal, the expression of humanity through oneness.

Remember that the rule of friendship is to be real. You are in the driver seat, steering and driving toward your destination of positivity instead of negativity! If your single and want to hook up with a friend. Hook up! There nothing wrong with it. Well! If you're young have fun and enjoy life. We all got certain preferences of men and women we like. It's not like we're out here sleeping around with everybody we meet. No! That's not what I'm saying. Keep in mind the 30-60-90-day rule. I'm saying when you have a special friend and you look at them in that way take a risk, have fun and enjoy the moments. But be cautious and prepared because sometimes the other person could just see you as just friends. And you must deal with it. Learning how to control your feelings and attraction toward a friend is key here. I have master controlling my feelings from being hurt, heartbroken and it left me in so much pain. That I now know how to take risk, turning my emotions/feelings off and on.

Yes! Friendship is a priceless gift, which you cannot buy. So, if you value your friendship and do not want to break that bond. Then I wouldn't recommend dating your friends. Real friendship is developed over time. You have two people who share a strong attachment with a bond of mutual understanding, trust and respect for each other, which in that shows how friendship is develop. But be cautious! Anyone who's been in the game of love a while, probably has a tale of sleeping around with one or two of their friends. Even if your friends and you remain friends after doing the deed, sex definitely should not changes things. Remember you are steering and driving toward your destination of positivity instead of negativity. You know what I think it is? People are afraid of rejection. Let's be adults about it. Rejection isn't the only response, but it does rear its ugly head every now and then controlling us. Leaving you dumb founded as the friend, of not being able to understand what happen to a connection you tried to make with your best friend, but you didn't see that it was simply platonic. Keep in mind that rejection will not happen to every potential friend or person you meet. But you do have to put yourself out there occasionally, but only when you're ready of course. I just suggest that you do it with maybe a close friend, that you feel my have that same attraction towards.

Faith already brought you two together and your friends already understand you, accept you, and bring out the best in you. You both are adults and have grown so close together that you now connected on many levels as if it is a potential soul mate. That's just my opinion, while speaking on love and compatibility of friends and how it creates a new level of understanding between two close friends, simply by looking at their star sign and how compatible they are in certain areas of life with someone. Maybe my view may consider you to view them as a potential maker of a relationship compatibility as it relates to love, social activities and sexual connectedness as well as appreciate the strengths and challenges of love using the zodiac star signs compatibility.

But Hey! I'm no match maker. I'm here to speak the truth and be real and honest as a friend. Everyone is in control of their own destiny. It's about understanding the plan God has for us. Some people might get their heart broken. Which means there weak. Love is not for the weak, but people seem to be weak before the presence of love. Which shows that you're not ready for love yet. We all got to go through obstacles and hurdles to get what we really want in the end. Just don't, stray too far from home to see that your soul mate could be that friend next to you. Best friends can be life partners. There is no doubt about that. If you want to be in a relationship. People might say a million different things. Worst case scenario, if you hook up with your best friend to see if you're a compatible match and it so happens does not work out, but you guys decided to stay friends. Then you two should still be friends because you both have that strong connection and bond to go back to friends. Even I have had a few friends that I may have hook up with. I'm still friends with some and others I have let go. Not all friendships last forever, in fact only about one in twelve friends end up being lifetime friends. And even those friendships must change and become something new many times over, as we all go through various life stages

We all want love. But love isn't perfect. It dam for sure, not a fairytale out of a storybook that always come easy with a happy ending. Love is overcoming obstacles, facing challenges, fighting to be together, holding on and never letting go. It is a short word, easy to spell, difficult to define, and impossible to live without. Love is work, but most of all, love is realizing that every hour, every minute, every second of it was worth it because you did it together.

Call me a hopeless romantic. But open your heart, open your mind. Love is used in many ways. It feels good to talk to somebody about things were concerned about. It's good to be able to trust somebody. We can be great friends with someone if we choose to make the effort. Not everyone has to be close friends, but it's integral to our happiness that we show people who we truly are, allow ourselves to know them and in return, remind each other through actions small or large that we care. We never need to be or feel alone in this world, but it's up to us to create and allow opportunities to be together, enjoy each other and be there for each other. It's up to us to make our relationships priorities. Hey! Just be a true friend who's loyal, kind and listen. Be fun and light. Be serious when needed, love extensively and forgive always.

MOVING FORWARD- END NOTES

Don't be scare to tell each other the truth, no matter how difficult it may be.

MOVING FORWARD- END NOTES

No matter what happens. Staying focus can help you accomplish almost anything. Sometimes you must lose to win again. Especially the next time you start to question whether you will ever experience truelove or find a soul mate.

ADDICTIONS

Tick Tock, Tick Tock.
How I wish I could turn back life clocks.
He likes a little porn, and so do you.
He doesn't care how many partners you've had; its all in the past.
Do you know a cry for help when someone wants you to be supportive?
Are we all addicted to something?
Everybody has an addiction. But is it perfectly ordinary and hardly worth doing anything about?
What is the root of the addiction?
Why do some people become addicts, while others don't?
Addiction can turn a healthy individual into a complete mess.
There are many things that one can become addicted to.
Sex, gambling, food, drugs, internet, apps, alcohol that has you quickly spin out of control if you aren't careful.
But sex, love and porn addiction aren't just gay issues; rather, they are predominately male issues.
There nothing fair about having an addiction.
Everything is a lot more complicated now a days.
Life is full of challenges. Economic difficulties, serious illness, family problems and political unrest plague people daily.
And how you face those challenges that comes your way, says much about your character and who you are on the inside.

Tick Tock, Tick Tock
How I wish I could control this life's clock.
Sometimes people are indirectly influenced by the actions of other people.
They call it peer pressure that requires direct persuasion from the other person.
These days you never really know.

Because most of our relationships start with sex before they turn into something substantial.
It can be rather difficult figuring out where exactly that line between the two is located.
Are you dating? Or are you just having sex?
Tick Tock, Tick Tock
How I wish I could turn back life's clock.
I'm not pointing fingers at the older generation for criticizing the young people for not knowing better.
I am ashamed that they can't step up to help educate and help to understand the risks and dangers they may have experience in our community.
Is it because of the way society has treated older guys that they seem so bitter and jaded?
They say life was simpler before, there was less to do, less to balance, there was fewer options, possibilities and choices to make.
Addiction has destroyed more dreams and hopes than you can imagine.
But what is the root cause of these symptoms.
Maybe it's the addiction to opinions of other people.
As a society we are addicted to what others think about us and how it their views affect us.
Maybe it's the addiction to the past and how people have an unhealthy attachment to events or situations that have occurred in the past.
Or maybe the addictions to worry and how the addiction is comprised of all the negative and self-defeating thoughts that make us anxious, disturbed, upset and stressed, that hold us back in life.
Each situation is unique. But why can't we stand up and help someone?

Tick Tock, Tick Tock
How I wish I could turn back life's clock.
Tick Tock, life clock is ticking.

And it require will power and determination to overcome that.
Overcome what holds us back from living to our fullest potential.
Hardest part of addiction recovery is admitting your problem.
These diagnoses are as widespread and problematic among straight men and bi-sexual men as they are among gays.

Tick Tock, Tick Tock.
Listen to me. Communication is the key.
Why it happens is unclear.
Can you admit that you have a sex addiction?
Typical behavior include compulsive masturbation, persistent use of pornography, exhibitionism, voyeurism, extreme acts of lewd sex and failure to resist sexual impulses.
Dam! That's kinky. My bad, I'm sorry. My thoughts almost got dominated by your sexual activity.
Your sexual addiction.
Everybody is addicted to something.
This is not a good thing and it helps neither addicts themselves.
An addiction isn't something that crops up overnight.
But you must admit you have a problem and face it head on.
Tick Tock, Tick Tock, Tick Tock, Tick Tock.
Tick Tock, life clock is ticking.

Chapter Ten

Rule#10. The New Rule to Online Dating from mistakes made and lessons learned.

Online dating can be fun. It can also be a little scary or even dangerous. Dating in general is usually an extremely risky matter because an individual always invests their time and money over a larger duration of time, to try to get recognize by somebody who may or may not be the correct match for them. Internet dating places is not a genuine place to find a perfect love or match. And if you do, you're lucky.

I have met my share of men online, and I have developed a few rules that I follow when it comes to meeting these men from these social sites too. From the genuine few I met through all the fake profiles filled with lies, I discover that we really had nothing in common. No real chemistry and a lot of judgements. And when you finally hook-up and go on a date they're horrible. Now, I didn't just make up these rules, they came from mistakes made and lessons learned from my own experiences. Now I've only seen two couples that found love online. Which is horrible, because as a black man we need more representation. But many of us spend most of our time fighting against a racial and social injustice system trying to survive. Having no time to take a moment to address the personal experience of trauma and toxic stress that it cause and its potential to create social, emotional and cognitive impairment. But let's keep it real. These online sites and apps use like A4A, BGC, Grindr etc. are not use for finding love. They are simply hookup sex sites for people that are DL/Bisexual men who some, not all, have unprotected sex with other HIV infected men from what I've gather. I'm not saying everyone on the sites and apps are doing it and are HIV positive. But from my experience I have encounter, some people are not living in their truth. They are just there for sex and are not open and honest discussing their HIV status and sexuality. Putting themselves and others in so much danger. Which probably explain why Black Americans, particularly black gay men has such a high rate of HIV infection compared to the rest of the population. Maybe there not consistently using condoms and getting tested for STD's on a regular. And their using these Apps and Websites exposing a lot more partners too. Deep down we know there's a greater issue when dealing with toxic people like that. And it will take a lot to heal the greatest hurt from them.

But remember we all know what the basic ingredient for love is, so proceed at your own risk. Do you really thank that we will find real love from these online websites? Shit! With today's digital addiction and how technology keeps us hooked. Even when you meet someone, they feel the need to engage with their digital devices in our lives, even if it is inappropriate. Nowadays people want interpersonal attraction, someone to create and maintain love which involves validating communications between the person you meet on a variety of issues, including understanding, showing concern for the other personal and emotional needs, developing companionship, physical attractiveness, cultivating and nurturing, physical and emotional, intellectual, and spiritual well beings, respecting, supporting, forgiving, accepting and encouraging, expression of appreciation and attraction such as pleasure and fidelity, commitment, shared activities, and also the absence of controlling, defensiveness, contempt, stonewalling and blaming among other factors. But to get what we really want; we need both face to face interactions that includes verbal and nonverbal communication that will allow one person to give to and receive from the other.

Don't get me wrong, I have no problem with online dating, I just have a problem with weak men. See what I want is a real man. Someone that knows their worth and value and has a strong moral compass. Someone who is considerate and able to communicate their feelings, without letting their insecurities dominate their psyche. See I'm a man who knows what I want and when I want it, and what I want is a real man who goes for what they want. Not a boy who may have somewhat of an idea or think too much about it and even if he does, he doesn't exert much effort to get it. I don't want a boy who is passive, but a man who is more assertive. Seems like to me you can't find real men anymore. And it's even harder when you're online looking because not everyone is honestly looking for a relationship. Maybe these social networking sites should promote online sex hookups instead of a platform for people with good hearts yearning for some love and warmth in their lives. Let's face it, not everyone will find a partner through online dating and be made an eternal love story. There will always be pros and cons to online dating. But one of my biggest mistakes and lesson learn from online dating is a long-distance relationship. I can't stand lack of durability. Not everyone is lucky enough to find someone from their own city. Even if you do, of course you first must interact online and then meet. And this is the most vital stage of bonding. Because you must spend time together in person to have an emotional connection. Shit! Not just emotional, but also physically. You must feel some form of true chemistry to be mentally bonded and psychologically to understand each other. Without this you have nothing, and the relationship cannot go a long way. From mistakes made and lesson learns I can't do a long-distance relationship. With the last guy I was dating I discover he was seeing someone else online he met, and I felt I was being used. Don't forget my 30-60-90-Day Rule. Yes, you are obligated to date multiple people, including online dating. But with him I felt like I was just another pawn used like a free vacation spot. Maybe he view us as strictly an online relationship and it was all about sex when he travel to meet me. But with all we communicated maybe something got lost in translation. Or maybe he use me to get to other single guys in the area near me. He always said he had other friends in the area he would go meet but never introduce me to. I'm not crazy. I'm not a fucking idiot or robot too. I love things like face to face human interaction and intimacy. Those things will never go out of fashion to me. Its mistakes made, and lesson learned regardless of how many times we spoke on the phone or text. Our first meeting had to be casual. It's my proof to see if the person I've been chatting with was a real person and didn't provide a fake profile online. I believe in comfort and safety. It can be nerve wracking when you meet someone for the first time. And I suggest a place like Star Bucks, because it's cheap and public and there is little stress and expectations. I don't prefer bars or clubs because it's too loud to talk and there are so many risks you can run into. Especially being around other men who are single themselves and on the prowl. Keep in mind this your first meeting to see each other and to get to know each other more. But let's keep it real, if you want to risk having your potential man out in public so people can get jealous and try to take him away from you, because he's a cute man and they can't control their hormones. Do it at your own risk? Test the waters, maybe it's faith to be together or not. Just because sex is your primary motivation for some, don't you forget about getting to know the person first. Because, going on a few dates and getting to know the person puts you under no obligation to sleep with them first, so have some decorum. This goes for people seeking a causal relationship as well. If you want to explore sex in a mutually respectful way, but not in an emotional way, you need to find someone who also wants to do the same thing. Find a person who likes to have sex and don't care and not seeking a serious relationship. That can be simple by stating your intentions up front in your first online meeting.

Public announcement to my DL/Bi-sexual men. Keep it moving and pass me by if you see me on one of the online profiles. Why are you even on the sites if you're DL &

closeted, because selling yourself is already awkward for real people like me looking for love. So, who has the time to put up with a whole a lot of effort into figuring out these closet queens? These sites should demand that people show a full body picture not just your face shot. They should make it mandatory that they express if there looking for a relationship or hook up. Because expressing confidence is what makes you sexy to me. So, I would like someone to show themselves off regardless of your body type. I like someone that's sweet and not afraid to show themselves as a man, which means basically describe yourself and your hobbies please. That's what I what and I'm more drawn to a positive word profile. Not the recent breakups about your ex or your mental health issues toward people. You can save those deeper and darker issues for your counselor, because I'm not in the business of saving lives and establishing that type of connection with someone. Don't get me wrong, I'm all about empowerment but not for these online dating sites for men. This is not a site where we gather to help others out with their serious sex addiction, drug problems or whatever. We are not professionals connected with the business trying to save souls, we're looking for love. Beside it's too much oversharing for me. Let's go back to the 30-day rule. Remember the risky territory, considering the no expectation period. If you bring baggage into the relationship it causes relationship problems down the road and let's face it, dating is already emotional and confusing world wind. Why would I want to step into that mess? See when we discuss the 30-60-90-day rule for the LGBT community its common mistakes we make, because as uncomfortable as it maybe be, we are under the microscope every day and judge by our looks. Yes, looks do matter, although it's stereotyping to size people up based on their looks. But snap judgements in the gay community about people is crucial to the way we function, even when there in the wrong. Let's makes some since of this. When people don't fit our preconceived notions, we tend to ignore the contradictions until they are too dramatic to overlook. And that was my biggest mistake and lesson learn. I was so busy worrying about the online appearance and how people thought of me, that I lost my way. I thought my attractiveness would reinforce or lure the right men to me, well the good ones anyway, if I control my appearance such as clothing, cosmetics, hairstyling a healthy diet and regular exercise. But I now realize that we can't control people. Sometimes I came off a little needy. A common mistake we make attaching ourselves too much and too quickly. There nothing wrong with having a good heart, but we as gay men needs to have our own voice, identity and our own life. So, don't latch on too quickly to run the risk of pushing a great guy away.

Look I can go on and on with this online dating. But all I can say is used it at your own risk, because there have been mistakes and lessons learned from it from my experience. And with today's technology and smartphones, they have transformed many aspect of our society, including how people seek out and establish romantic relationships. And trust me I'm not the only one who have had bad experience from these social sites. I realize that online dating is entirely different. Without going into sexual orientation dynamics and gender politics, I know that gay men are sexually active in the dating world. You're likely to hit up a profile that's in an open relationship status in the first 10 profiles you sift through online. I guess they say we're men and that some men really like to bone. But that doesn't mean we shouldn't go without having a sense of decorum, because we're no different from straight dating world. We must tell ourselves what we're looking for and to be honest about it. And you must be comfortable to share it on your profile to get what you want. Don't flirt and bring up things upon which you won't act. Let me say this I have learned a lot about myself when I was doing the online dating thing. If nothing else, online dating helps you realize how to be a better human being. So, if you put out negative, you get negative back. But as I stated in the beginning if you prefer online dating. Use it at your own risk.

MOVING FORWARD- END NOTES

Dating is pressure and tension. What is a date, really but a job interview that lasts all night? Use that time to find out who you are and who others are.

MOVING FORWARD QUESTION.

Are you more open or selective when it comes to your relationship? Should there be a balance of both?

MOVING FORWARD QUESTION.

How would you rate your relationship of how effective you both are at communicating with each other?

SCARED

My anxiety kicks in.
This walk to those double doors seem so long.
Which had me feeling symptoms of Dizziness. Shortness of breath.
A sudden fear came over me.

My thoughts in my mine spin out of control.
Why does it feel like I'm walking to meet death?
All it is. Is a checkup. Better late than never.

But this distractions can't make me forget.
The terrible mistake I made.
Unprotected sex with the one I thought I love.
I can't relax. I can't eat. I can't sleep.
Hearing the Doctor call my name to come in.
It's time for the test. To go in and be tested.
Let me say it out loud. To help me cope with my anxiety and depression.
For AIDS/HIV or any other diseases.
To grab back hold of my life.

So much stress on my mind.
Tightness in my chest. Having this constant fear that death is right here beside me.
For all who passed the test, be bless.
I know this is not what I deserve because of a horrible mistake I made.

But it has me feeling weak and worthless.
With no one by myside. I'm hear standing alone, without the one I thought loved me.
No matter how nice of a guy I am. I'm always alone.
I'm always giving them love, putting them first, giving them my heart. I broke all the rules while loving them.

Look at me now, standing here alone.
Hell yeah! I'm scared. Tomorrow is never promise.
I've always been on the grind, hustling to survive.
There's no stopping me now. What's done is done right?
I'll find the way to see the light through the darkness.
With counseling, medication our survive.
The strongest always survive.
Even from the demons with those negative voices that whisper to me daily.

Taking baby steps with breaths of encouragement to get through this life.
But not everyone is so lucky to have survive to tell their story.
Not everyone is blessed with mental and moral support.
They suppressed their emotion to keep from severely hurting themselves or living in their truth. Knowing that doing so is not healthy.
Life goes on, right? Somebody got to pay my fucking bills.
A hand dealt, a decision I made and must live with for the rest of my life right.

Everything has a purpose.

So, let's help the next person by raising awareness on the issues to not make the mistakes I made.
One of the biggest part of compassion is respecting people's privacy.
Don't pry about someone's medical status or personal medication information and make sure people around you understand that's it's not okay to do that.
Don't force people with HIV to talk about how they feel or what they're dealing with.
Just be there for them, if they want to talk.
Pressure makes people uncomfortable.
When the time comes, I won't people to remember I was here on earth to make a difference regardless of my mistakes.

My life still has value, meaning and purpose.
When the time comes to move on. I won't my last words to stay in the hearts of those I loved and touch.
Safer sex is all about protecting yourself. Be prepared.
It doesn't have to be a passion killer.
Live life the way you are supposed to. Not wasting a lifetime worrying about death. If you do make a mistake. Its ok!
Instead fill each day with as much joy as possible.
But join our brother & sisters in the fight for a cure.
Continue to live out loud, because life is a celebration.
Remember this is not the end of your story, but it is the start of a comeback for a new beginning.
And once you recognize and start living in your truth, you can begin to write a new story.

Chapter Eleven

Rule#11. It's not a rule, but a guide to understanding a lack of awareness on all diseases.

There is an exception to this rule. I believe in the forgiveness of sin and the redemption of ignorance. A lack of awareness is perhaps one of the most challenging barriers in this world today. It keeps people from seeking the care that they need. It keep policy makers from building systems that prevent and treat people. It limits the flow of reasons needed to address the lack of capacity. It prevent families from having a lack of insight awareness on illness that leads to dark secrets of people committing suicide or suffering from (PTSD) Post Traumatic Stress Disorder, which means they probably was exposed to one or more traumatic events in life, such as sexual assault, warfare, serious injury or disease, or threats of imminent death that result in feelings of increase fear, horror and powerlessness. It causes a fear of Phobia that prevents people from being tested for all diseases. It even keeps people from mending a broken heart, getting over a fear of love and learning to love yourself. Fear will make you think you will never find true love. I don't want to call this a rule, but a guide to understanding a lack of awareness on all diseases. There are a lot diseases out there to talk about. But the disease I do want to focus on is HIV/AIDS. Which stands for human immunodeficiency virus. It is the virus that can lead to acquired immunodeficiency syndrome, or AIDs. Unlike some other viruses, the human body cannot get rid of HIV. That means that once you have HIV, you have it for life.

Right now, no safe and effective cure currently exist, but scientists are working hard to find one, and remain hopeful. Meanwhile, with proper medical care, HIV can be controlled. The treatment option for HIV can help people living with HIV experience long and production lives. So, I encourage everyone to get tested. Getting an HIV test is the only way to know if you have HIV. HIV is spread mainly through anal or vaginal sex or by sharing drug use equipment with an infected person.

Being diagnosed HIV positive can be devastating to have and deal with, but it is not necessarily a death sentences, nor something you need to cope with on your own. These are emotions that we will inevitably feel and will have to manage. This is what you must tell yourself every day to never forget. But this can be hard especially when you have what I like to call bullies around you. People are always

going to point fingers and talk about you until the day we die. But let them bitches talk, they not paying your bills. All they are to me are bullies and people with insecurities.
There is no doubt that victims of bullying are subjected to stressful situations. Whether they are threated, cyberbullied on these social network sites, or experience name calling in public, these types of bullying leave lasting effects. And after prolonged exposure of bullying can start to develop adverse reactions. Some victims of bullying will experience depression, eating disorders, and even thoughts of suicide. They can also develop anxiety disorders, (PTSD) Post-Traumatic Stress Disorder, generalized anxiety disorder, panic attacks, and social anxiety disorders.
No one wants to be humiliated or be seen negatively by others, this leads to a social anxiety disorder. Having self-consciousness everyday with the fear that others will judge them for not being able to live in their truth. And you know it's what people do. They ridicule or bully people behind closes doors or in public with harsh words or stares. I hear people making slick comments all the time. And it hurts. People don't understand that when we as people face crisis every day in our lives. We all resort to family support and our community, for help or answers for our problems, when the stress of life problems, blinds us from seeing the

solution ourselves to fix. When we don't have support from either of the two. It leads to serious problems adding on to the baggage we already have. I can admit to my truth. With all that I had going on in my life, I did not have anyone out there who I could confine to for advice. I wasn't close to my family at the time to get support I needed to help me battle my depression. I did not have any true friends to talk to everyday or call at any time. I was living a very lonely existence life and needed help. I could not count the many times I thought of committing suicide, but the number of attempts I had tried was two, but they were failed attempts. For some reason maybe it was God being there in spirit every time to stop me. All I know he would send some stranger in my life to talk me out of it every time. Whether they were a person passing through with a message into my life for the moment.

But love makes you do crazy things. I don't know what I was thinking at the time. Especially living in the moment with alcohol involved, not thinking having unprotected sex for the first time with the one I thought I love, even if it was only one time that lead to being HIV positive. I rather I tell you my side of the story, than here it from some horses ass mouth who did not experience it themselves. Life sometimes delivers the unexpected. And people will look down upon thee, not knowing your battles and judge you about your life that they're not living. Yes! That's to be expected. But God will be the only person I face for my sins. I know that he is a loving, kind and compassionate being, which is why I forgive those bad people for labeling me and judging me for whatever mistakes I may have made and for my outsides circumstances I face in life.

You know there is a stigma of dating someone who is HIV positive. Just having the disease can feel like social suicide. Which certainly aren't the best version of our culture, but any homosexual can attest to the reality of some sects of our society who view people's HIV status like designer labels. When it comes to negative men choosing to date people like me who's positive, it runs the risk of someone confusing their Prada suit in a Marshall's bag. There was a time in my life when I had the nerve to put myself back out to date. I met this one guy who knew that rumors didn't transmit the virus and that the potential for a loving relationship was worth a few whispers over a mismatched label, so I thought. When it comes to the rules of dating, I believe you have a choice to talk about your status. Because technically you are in the beginning stages of getting to know someone. But to live in your truth, you should be truthful if you can handle it.

HIV stigma doesn't only affect those carrying the virus. It affects your partner as well. The gay community or even society is quickly to judge you on your mistakes and place shame on anyone who deviates from the boundaries of pluses and minuses. If you are lucky to find a special person in your life hold on to them. But keep your personal life private from the world. Its nobody business but yours. A private life is a happy life. Regardless if you found them from online, clubs, bars, grocery stores, churches or general hook ups through mutual friends. There are always going to be pros and cons in finding love regardless of where you find it at. Privacy for me just decreases the drama, bad luck, bullshit, and insecurities in your life period. But you must have the strength and courage to handle whatever life throws at you.

What I want to do is reduce the stigma in the private life of someone like myself living with the status and how important it is to take steps to promote the empowerment of oneself to find support and resources needed that will help me and others in their time of need. In order to do that we have to keep pushing the issue of negative attitudes on Gay, Bisexual and other men who have sex with men. Because it is discrimination and were being treated unfairly which affects our health and well-being negatively. And such barriers that affect our health must be addressed at different levels of society because every life is worth keeping.

My story is something I don't normally talk about because I do live a private life and I like to stay to myself. But I wanted to share and tell my story, my truth. I did meet him online. A known dating app. We met, started to hang out and get to know each other. You know we didn't have sex in the beginning, which was a great thing. He gave me the impression that he was a nice genuine guy. We went through the 90 days process, almost a year. But for all I knew he could have been contracted the virus from someone else and either he knew he had it or didn't know. But as time went on and having fun and getting to know each other. One night out and about at the club having fun. Clearly, I wasn't thinking and every love and sex comments he made to me was lies of love, but it had me hook. We both was drunk on alcohol, me drunk in love and him high off weed, not thinking making a foolish mistake that night. Having unprotected sex that night change my life forever. A mistake I must relive and remember ever day of my life to stay alive. It's a struggle and life changing. That's how I found out I was positive. Me! Who's always safe but made this one foolish mistake. The day I was tested had my hold world felt upside down, I had no one and nowhere to run to, no family support because it was and still is a secret to them. Not knowing who to talk too weighed heavy on my soul. People don't understand hearing the message that we are unworthy, evil, filthy and worst sinners ever to walk this earth affects how we view ourselves? I believe homophobia at home and in our community is dangerous because if affects how gay men and bisexual men see themselves. Affecting our feelings of self-worth and consequently the choices we make in life. I personally do not attend churches on a weekly basis for my own reasons. I refuse not to put myself through it. I worship and celebrate God at home now. I'm still trying to decide if there's a God with the shit I been through. The most important thing in my life right now is inner peace, so I tend to get rid of things which upset that balance. My story is not written to offend anyone but to show that this is an issue that needs to address. It all starts at home and in our community. We should be teaching people about the lack of awareness on diseases and groups of same gender attractions. Teach people how to live in their truth without fear. Helping them understand all diseases and views on different religious groups and that casting gays out of churches is discrimination against their beliefs system. We should be protecting the rights of every individual regardless of religion, sex or etc. Jesus himself was not about judging. I personally can care less on all these temples of God being built every day, to bring his children he created together to teach us in his ways. Which is to be kind, loving and compassionate towards one another? In my opinion we don't need houses or temples to dwell in. The entire universe is God house.

Just keep in mind love can make you do crazy things. And when there is a lot going on, depression distorts your thinking to the point where you're not perceiving reality properly. Looking back in my past I was damage goods at the time with a broken heart and crush spirit. I was looking to be filled with love with whomever I could get it from. I think my issues started from my childhood. Epiphany! I was always someone that craved love and attention when I was young. My parents was not always around. This is not to say that I accepted love that willingly. As you can imagine, my issues eliminated several potential friends and partners and I often found myself lonely and disappointed. The root of my inability to accept and find love easily stems back to my childhood. Growing up my mother and father was unable to connect with me. Which has me now disguising my pain in front of people with jokes to laugh to keep from crying. Only releasing my tears behind closed doors, hating myself even more. I was terrified. Later, in the years I found myself trying to build a connection with anyone that came along. But all it did was cause me to have this fear, an overwhelming sense of failure as if I was being judge by people. I just had a sense of spiritual emptiness in my heart that I was trying to fill. Maybe I was hurt, hiding from myself. I was vulnerable and in a negative state, but also stuck a crossroads trying to figure out how to change my life.

You must forgive to release to move forward. I made the decision that I will cast all my anxieties out. All my worries. All my concerns, once and for all on him my lord and savior Jesus. Trust in him to teach me what I need to know to change fear into faith. 1 Peter 5:7. Cast all your anxiety on him because he cares for you. God has a purpose for everything. God will never give you more than you can bear. He has now surrounded me with a support system to help prepare me for the next step. I have gained the full realization of emptiness and have fully awakened with a clear state of mind that has me understanding the truth of my emptiness. I realize now that I have made mistakes, but I must keep going by loving myself and putting myself first and maintain this meditation on the emptiness of the inherently existent self.

MOVING FORWARD-END NOTE

It's true that obstacles and suffering shapes us for greatness. If we run from it, you will never learn to face it. We can't control faith. But always remember its part of life.

MOVING FORWARD QUESTIONS.

Is there a set amount of time one should wait before they become intimate?

OBSTACLES

The blood of our ancestors.
Course fiercely through our veins.
We come from a place of old trouble times.
Even if we lighten the load. The end still seems so far.
Remember we do seem to repeat our mistakes repeatedly, but not indefinitely.
We are not responsible for the choices our parents, grandparents and ancestors made, but we are responsible for learning from their mistakes and using all experiences to make us and this world better.
Remember our family bond. Is what makes us stronger?
A family is like a building. You need a strong base to build one.
It's us against the world. All we have is each other.
Our obstacles and suffering shape us for greatness.
Only wisdom has the true power to cut our delusions from the root.
We are still connected to slavery and we can cure it.
Remember the legacy of slavery lingers in our cities ghettos.
Nevertheless, as anyone even vaguely aware of the social conditions in contemporary America.
Susceptible to stereotyping, stigmatized for their cultural styles, isolated socially, experiencing in internalized sense of helplessness and despair, with limited access to communal networks of mutual assistance.
Should Black Americans get slavery reparations?

Reparations are a restitution for slavery.
An apology and repayment to black citizens whose ancestors were forced into the slave trade.
Shit! Pay me. Let's point to these historic inequalities as reasons for current schisms between white and black Americas when it comes to income, housing, healthcare and incarceration rates.
Look at the timeline for Slavery in the US, a case in arguing for reparations.
We shall overcome. I do believe. If we fight to change it.
The struggle to change the world is a long one.
We cannot change the world till we change hearts, and we cannot change hearts of others until our own hearts are transformed.
So, let today be a day for change. In our way of living.
Be free and happy; let us rejoice in the music.
Feel it, hear it, and dance to it.
The rhythm of the old slave drums.
Let it go. Cast out whatever it is, that keeps us from lighten the load to live.
Never forget, your love is the key.
Families are changing, but still they are the key to happiness.
Unresolved issues can keep us from overcoming obstacles.
But if you explore the challenges and barriers you can achieve your dreams.

LIFE ON PAGES

Transported through time.
Only to come across you Black Bird.
I'm no Alice in Wonderland, I can see straight through the looking glass.
The feeling of hopelessness signifies you are experiencing conflict with your spirituality.
Connecting with spiritual beings, communicating through the sounds of harmony.
It implies that you are not following your desired path in life.
Following our own rhythm is parallel to following our hearts.
Living our truth and being as authentic as we can be.

Black Bird, Black Bird, Black Bird. In the rose garden.
Through the eyes of the soul.
Imagine your soul cycle thumbling through blank pages.
Encountering spiritual beings.
Only to laugh, cry and heal through human experiences.

Imagine that you have this uncanny ability to see and understand.
What's beneath the different facades.
Seeing thousands of unseen memorable moments.
Just to connect with your life on pages.

We all go through struggles and experience hardship, battles in our lives.
Always asking for a chance that's fair and equal to our stride.
No one knows what will happen in the future.
Some are not here to enjoy. Life is hard, life is difficult, but when its good enjoy it.
We're all trying to discover that map of our own calling.
But be cautious.

Try not to fall down that rabbit whole.
This crazy wonderland may reveal deep thoughts.

Times a ticking. Tick Tock, Tick Tock.
I know my soul can't take much more.
Countless rejections. Too many blows to the heart.
Walking unprotected, with no armor through the Secret Garden.

Not off with his head. If not careful.
The Red Queen in this world is crazy.
She believe that the only truth that matters is what people believe.

No turning back. No rewinds.
Our souls will be destined and intertwine.
Manifest the love of your life with the law of attraction.
Who needs the Queen?
At the beginning of every great story, before anything exciting happens, we see something that looks a lot like a fairy tale life, your fairy tale.

We all have a list of traits we want our soulmate to have.
What if Mr./Mrs. Right has been here the whole time.
I'll be loving the way he filled me with knowledge.
The way that books could never do.
I want to draw in suitors like Kings, Princes, and lords.
Swarming in largely by the hoards.
And when the right one catches my eye.
Even when were apart. My soul can feel their presence.
It will stretch on for miles and miles.

Experiencing ups and downs twist and turns.
Only to laugh, cry and heal through human experience with you.
This story can go on and on.

But it appears on paper as black. Maybe it's written in disappearing ink.

Tick Tock, Tick Tock.
The rabbit on another mission and down the rabbit whole goes.
My pursuit to meet him have gone astray.
Maybe he has answers I need about my life.
Perhaps I'm not as strong as everyone thought.

Black Bird, Black Bird, Black Bird.
Love is something you create, not an emotion that arises out of thin air.
Time a ticking, Tick Tock, Tick Tock.
Are you living life to the fullest or just merely living?
Once you start living. Your life will appear on the blank pages.

Dear Me

This is a letter to my future self. I'm writing because this will remind me not to forget. How the United States is a fast-becoming divided society. For some we are already fighting the good fight, that of discrimination and our future is being based on race, and not on experience & education. But even sad, when society is divided among each other. Almost in a form of cliques that have people afraid to talk about it. Yes, I said it. I was raised to be tough and to not take anything from anyone. I spent my hold life trying to please and impress. But all it did was make me hate myself even more for it. When I thought I found someone who I thought I loved. Someone to love me back, even with all my issues, I lost them. Found Love, Lost Love. It change me. Love is torn apart for them now and me apart with it. I had wanted to die because I could not be who I wanted to be. I could not be who they wanted me to be. But I could not die either, any more than I could live. My mind, my body and my soul is tired. I'm tired. I realize that this place is not going anywhere, and the people are not going to change. People holding me down and back from me being me. But there is power in the name Jesus. I'm starting to break through these chains. I'm starting to come to terms with me. I can't hold back my breath anymore. No more secrets that made me unhappy. So, I'm going to try something new. Like living and telling the truth giving love a try again slowly. My name is Kenneth Brown and I am gay veteran of the US Army. I'm still fighting to find my place in this world. So many struggles I had faced. Dealing with ones sexuality, while developing an identity for oneself. Everyone wants to feel love, comfortable and accepted. But this road I'm traveling on has no ordinary journeys. I know what I face on the way, will empower me and teach me to encourage others. Sometimes there are days, I may look and feel defeated, but don't count me out yet. I still haven't given up. With what little faith I have left, I will make it. My way, the honest way.

MOVING FORWARD -ENDNOTE

I had a habit of letting my torn heart get the best of me. Pushing my potential soul mate right pass me. There nothing wrong in looking deep into your life to reflect and heal from it. By doing so, you will see that you may have felt vulnerable and taken advantage of by demons at times soul searching for life purpose.

Made in the USA
Columbia, SC
04 July 2025